Library of
Davidson College

Political Theory and Political Philosophy

Seventeen Volumes of Previously Unavailable British Theses

Edited by
MAURICE CRANSTON
London School of Economics and Political Science

A Garland Series

The Problem of Liberalism in the Thought of John Stuart Mill

Neil Thornton

Garland Publishing, Inc., New York & London
1987

Copyright © 1987 by Neil Thornton
All rights reserved

Library of Congress Cataloging-in-Publication Data

Thornton, Neil, 1927–
The problem of liberalism in the thought of John
Stuart Mill.

(Political theory and political philosophy)
Originally presented as the author's thesis (Ph. D.)—
University of London.
Bibliography: p.
1. Mill, John Stuart, 1806–1873—
Contributions in political science. 2. Liberalism. I. Title.
II. Series.
JC223.M66T49 1987   320'.01   86-27064
ISBN 0-8240-0831-6

All volumes in this series are printed
on acid-free, 250-year-life paper.

Printed in the United States of America

THE PROBLEM OF LIBERALISM IN THE THOUGHT OF JOHN STUART MILL

N.S. Thornton

"The first question in regard to any man of speculation is, what is his theory of human life? In the minds of many philosophers, whatever theory they have of this sort is latent, and it would be a revelation to themselves to have it pointed out to them in their writings as others can see it, unconsciously moulding everything to its own likeness."

— J.S. Mill: "Bentham"

Thesis submitted for the Ph.D. degree in the University of London

ABSTRACT

Mill aimed to formulate a positive and individualistic liberalism setting out the conditions of a pluralistic, democratic society. Each individual in such a society would strive to realise personal ideals within the framework of a common social morality; the majority would accord critical deference to an elite of the most cultivated. (Chapter I)

Mill revises Bentham's conception of morality by arguing for the central moral importance of self-culture. Bentham's crucial inadequacy was his overlooking the moral importance of character (learned dispositions), Mill thought. (Chapter II)

Mill's division of human conduct marks off severally the boundaries of the moral, the prudential, and the aesthetic. (Chapter III)

With the distinction between higher and lower pleasures, *Utilitarianism* embraces an explicit ethics of self-development. *On Liberty* links self-development with individuality. For the 'negative' concept of freedom Mill substitutes 'positive' individuality, a concept more adequate (within the context of the new mass society) to an account of liberty. Individuality is the same as self-determination. It is man's most important "permanent interest". (Chapters IV & V)

Mill's high valuation of tolerance is justified in part by his fallibilism. A corollary of his fallibilism is his concept of man's nature as essentially open. Yet his doctrine of individuality and self-development implies there are characteristics an individual of necessity has. A resolution of this apparent contradiction can be effected. (Chapter VI)

Mill relies upon a version of naturalism which combines the Greek doctrine of function with a certain meta-ethical principle. This latter involves an appeal to the experience of the 'experienced'. This mode of ethical justificiation is doubtfully reconcilable with his moral individualism. (Chapter VII)

R.B. Friedman has argued Mill believes only a minority to be capable of self-determination. This view runs counter to my account of Mill's theory of progress but will not withstand detailed examination. (Chapter VIII)

Shirley Letwin and Maurice Cowling have argued that Mill's 'high-minded' liberalism leads him into political paternalism, but their interpretations cannot be sustained. (Chapter IX)

"Permanent" interests are correlative with rights and hence with the rules of justice. Just as Mill is concerned to demand absolute immunity from interference for *self*-regarding conduct, so he is prepared to argue conversely that an important part of other-regarding conduct, namely *unjust* other-regarding conduct, requires absolutely to be controlled. (Chapters X & XI)

TABLE OF CONTENTS

Chapter   **Page**

       ABSTRACT..1
       TABLE OF CONTENTS................................3
       INTRODUCTION...7

PART I

LIBERAL FOUNDATIONS

I.   MILL AND HIS TIME:
      THE CENTRAL PROBLEMS FOR LIBERALISM 10

      Problematic approach 10
      Moral Individualism in a Transitional Age 13
      The Function of Social Philosophy 17
      The Three 'Levels' of Mill's Liberalism 19

II.   UTILITY AND MORAL INDIVIDUALISM 21

      Happiness and Self-Development 21
      Morality and Individual Character 23
      Morality and Consequences 26
      The Two Parts of Morality 27
      Morality and Legislation 31

III. MORALITY AND INDIVIDUAL IDEALS 35

      Morality and the Ideal of Individual Development 35
      Mill's Three-Fold Division of Human Conduct 38

IV.	SELF-DEVELOPMENT AND INDIVIDUALITY	42

Happiness and Self-Development 42
Self-Development and Individuality 46
Criteria for Individuality 48
Individuality, Self-Determination
    and Relative Difference...51

V.	INDIVIDUALITY, FREEDOM AND THE TYRANNY OF THE MAJORITY	53

Negative and Positive Freedom 53
Individuality as Self-Development? 61
Self-Determination and Free Will 63
Individuality and Self-Development 64
Self-Development as the Ultimate End 67

VI.	FALLIBILISM, INDIVIDUALITY AND THE OPENNESS OF HUMAN NATURE	69

Liberalism and Fallibilism 69
Individuality and the Openness of Human Nature 72

VII.	THE JUSTIFICATION OF LIBERALISM	77

The Justification of Liberalism 77
Fact, Value and Moral Individualism 80
On the Distinction Between Art and Science 81
Aristotelianism and Justification 84
The Proof of an Ultimate End 85
The Appeal to Competent Judges 88
Self-Development and the Autonomy of Morals 96

PART II

THE SCOPE AND LIMITS OF LIBERTY

VIII. SELF-DEVELOPMENT, PROGRESS AND THE FREEDOM OF THE MAJORITY............99

   Self-Development and Progress 99
   Education and Goodness 100
   Progress and the Freedom of the Majority 105
   Friedman Conflates Two Distinct Theses 110

IX. NEGATIVE LIBERALISM AND HIGH-MINDED LIBERALISM.........................119

   Benthamite Liberalism 119
   High-Minded Liberalism 124
   Letwin on Mill's Doctrine of Self-Perfection
      and on the Role of the Elite...126
   Political Paternalism 131
   The Essay on Liberty
      and the Domination of the Elite..................................132
   Is Liberalism Essentially Authoritarian? 139

X. THE SCOPE AND LIMITS OF LIBERTY 146

   Pluralistic Liberalism 146
   The Reception of Mill's Principle 150
   The Sphere of Liberty 151
   The Principle of Self-Protection 153
   Interests and Rights 154
   Mill's Doctrine of Interests 158
   Mill on Interests and Rights 161

| XI. | THE PRINCIPLE OF SELF-PROTECTION ....168 |

Utility and Permanent Interests 168
Permanent Interests, Rights and Self-Protection 170
The Self-Regarding Excluded from Morality 173
The Other-Regarding Coextensive
 with Moral Conduct 176
Justice and Other-Regarding Conduct 177

BIBLIOGRAPHY 184

INTRODUCTION

The controlling purpose of my thesis is to consider the problem of liberalism as it shapes the thought of John Stuart Mill. The problem is to formulate a 'positive' liberalism which takes self-development as the highest moral and political value. The basis of this problem is Mill's recognition that it is impossible to formulate a defensible 'negative' liberalism taking non-interference as the highest value. Underlying any claim to freedom from interference will be some reference (explicit or implicit) to that on behalf of which immunity from coercion is being claimed. Thus, lying behind Mill's advocacy of non-interference is the positive aspect of his liberalism - what John Plamenatz has called the 'high-minded' strand in his liberalism. What Mill is demanding freedom *for* is individuality and self-development. And involved in his notions of individuality and self-development is a certain concept of man, of his distinctive needs and potentialities. In terms of this general schema of the structure of Mill's liberalism, the various problems discussed in the following chapters can be seen to be nested within the central problem.

Is Mill a Liberal?

John Stuart Mill has long been thought of as one of the greatest of English liberal thinkers. But now, after more than a century, his liberal reputation is being seriously challenged. Recent interpretations of Mill's political thought have focussed on its perfectionist strain, stressing that he valued negative liberty less for its own sake than as a condition of self-determination and self-development.[1] Moreover, some critics have concluded that because of his positivistic emphasis on consensus and on deference to an elite Mill was driven into an authoritarian or, at best,

---

[1] See especially M. Cowling, *Mill and Liberalism* (Cambridge, 1963); Shirley Robin Letwin, *The Pursuit of Certainty* (Cambridge, 1965); G. Himmelfarb (ed.) "Introduction" to *Essays on Politics and Culture* (New York, 1963); Currin V. Shields, "Introduction" to *On Liberty* (Indianapolis, 1956); J.B. Schneewind, "Introduction" to *Mill's Ethical Writings* (New York, 1965) and "Introduction" to *Mill's Essays on Literature and Society* (New York, 1965); John M. Robson, *The Improvement of Mankind* (London, 1968).

paternalistic position.[2] And one of the most discerning of Mill's recent critics has concluded that even though Mill must be judged one of the greatest of liberals, he did not succeed in setting out "a coherent, defensible liberal theory of the state which is different in principle from authoritarian, anti-liberal theories".[3]

A number of Maurice Cowling's charges against Mill have been ably rebutted by John Rees,[4] and Alan Ryan has replied to some of McCloskey's criticisms.[5] Rees, however, thinks there remains a serious problem as to whether it is possible to reconcile Mill's enthusiasm for the clerisy and for consensus with his commitment to liberty and individuality.

Recent revaluations of Mill's liberalism all raise in one form or another the question 'Was Mill a liberal?" Some answer 'Yes', others 'No'. My answer is 'Yes'; and my thesis is a sustained attempt to make that answer a convincing one. My purpose is two-fold; first, I try to bring closer to the surface certain philosophical, psychological, moral, sociological and historical assumptions which are at the basis of Mill's liberalism - but which he does not always succeed in making explicit. In developing and supporting a particular way of construing the main foundations of Mill's political philosophy - with special emphasis on his concept of man - I aim to establish that his philoopshy is indeed liberal. By setting out Mill's theory in such a way as to exhibit its major elements I hope to bring out his deep and abiding concern for individual liberty as the supreme value in morals and politics. Secondly, in the course of laying bare the main foundations of Mill's liberalism I shall be examining certain of the interpretations of a number of his most recent commentators and critics. My own reflections, of course, owe a lot to the writings of Mill's many critics, even where I cannot agree with their views. However, it has seemed to me that if I am to develop fully my own view, I cannot expend space on detailed critiques of more than

---

[2] Cowling, Letwin and Shields are the most notable representatives of this view.
[3] H.J. McCloskey, "The Problem of Liberalism", *The Review of Metaphysics*, Vol.19 (1965-66). See also "Mill's Liberalism", *The Philosophical Quarterly*, April 1963; "Mill's Liberalism - A Rejoinder to Mr. Ryan", *The Philosophical Quarterly* Vol.16, No.62 (1966).
[4] John Rees, "Was Mill for Liberty?", *Political Studies,* Vol.14 (1966).
[5] Alan Ryan, "Mr. McCloskey on Mill's Liberalism", *The Philosophical Quarterly,* Vo.14, No.56 (July, 1964).

a few of the most important of recent interpretations of Mill's liberalism. Thus I focus on those questions in current controversy that seem to me most in need of further discussion.

One or two further introductory remarks may be in place here. First, in expounding and interpreting Mill's liberalism I shall be picking out and developing what I take to be the main strands in his theory, so that my account does not aim at being comprehensive. Secondly, to achieve my purpose I need to provide a consistent way of understanding Mill and thus to bring out any notable examples of vagueness, obscurity, inconsistency or tension in his theory. In doing this I sometimes extrapolate from Mill's views, in directions where it seems useful to try to fill them out or (occasionally) to render them more coherent and defensible. Finally, no attempt is made to conceal my own attraction for Mill's kind of liberalism. My general procedure is to provide as careful an account of his central arguments as I can manage, while everywhere following the principle of generosity in interpretation: 'Always prefer an interpretation that preserves consistency where the case for a rival interpretation that would impute an inconsistency is inconclusive'.

PART I

LIBERAL FOUNDATIONS

CHAPTER I

MILL AND HIS TIME: THE CENTRAL PROBLEMS FOR LIBERALISM

Problematic Approach

Was Mill a liberal? This is the general problem with which I shall be concerned throughout the thesis. In assaying an answer to this question I shall adopt what has been called the "problematic" approach to the history of philosophy. "The first question the historian will ask himself about any philosopher is this: 'What problem was he trying to solve?' And then he will go on to ask himself such further questions as: 'How did the problem arise for him'? 'What new methods of tackling it did he use'?"[6] John Passmore's suggestion is that in order to understand a philosophical position "'we must retrace the steps of its construction, and accompany the mind of its author in its quest for the truth.' "[7] Adopting this suggestion, I shall use, in addition to Mill's standard theoretical writings, his *Autobiography* and (occasionally) his published letters as a useful guide to what he took to be the central problems for a liberal philosophy of politics. Not that I think Mill is always fully conscious of the nature of his problems or of the assumptions with which he was working. Looking back at Mill's liberalism from our vantage point it is of course possible to see it in ways not available to him. Thus we are better able to see it as a distinct contribution to an ongoing liberal tradition and can pick out more clearly

---

[6] John Passmore, "The Idea of a History of Philsophy", in *History and Theory*, Beiheft 5, 1965, p.29.
[7] Sir Henry Jones, in his Introduction to the English translation of *A History of the Problems of Philsophy* by Paul Janet and Gabriel Scailles (London 1902) p.xii. Quoted by Passmore, *Ibid*, p.27.

than could he the lineaments of the social milieu to which his liberalism was in part a response. Some appreciation of Mill's overriding purposes and of his intellectual and historical situation is a prerequisite of a proper undersanding of his liberalism. Unless we know something of those purposes we shall not fully understand the particular theoretical and practical problems his liberalism was designed to meet nor fully understand his answers to those problems.

In order to reach a better understanding of Mill's liberalism I shall occasionally take account of knowledge concerning his social and intellectual situation that was not fully available to him. But though it is necessary to recognise that Mill's situation influenced his purposes in ways of which he could not have been fully aware, Mill's own writings must remain our primary source for an understanding of his intellectual and social situation and of the controlling purposes underlying his liberalism. I shall almost always give the greatest weight to what Mill says about his own aims or purposes. Furthermore, my final interpretation will, it is hoped, be one that Mill himself would have been willing to accept as a fair account of the main lines of his thinking about liberty.

The aim of my thesis is to develop and support a way of construing the major themes in Mill's liberalism so that it can be seen to be structured according to an underlying unity. John Morley went straight to the point in saying that "the idea of perfectibility. . . . is the key alike of the *Liberty*, the *Utilitarianism* and some of the most original chapters on the Political Economy".[8] How to provide for progress towards individual self-development surely was the controlling purpose of Mill's liberalism. His liberalism was dominated by this nexus of problems: How to allow for the flourishing of the interconnected ideals of liberty, individuality and self-development within the overall framework of a democratic society, a society which would be unified by a widely accepted and deep attachment to the general welfare and would be ready to accept the intellectual and moral leadership of an educated elite. Mill's interest in promoting the common good and his conviction that moral and social progress largely depends upon a small number of exceptional and original individuals is not (as some critics maintain) incompatible with his liberalism. One main aim of my

---

[8] *Fortnightly Review*, Vol.xvi, 1874, p.648. Quoted by Shirley Robin Letwin, *op.cit.* p.300.

thesis is to show how Mill's interest in consensus and concern to establish the authority of a clerisy springs from the same liberal source that gives rise to his persistent and deeply felt belief in the freedom and dignity of the individual.

In developing my thesis I claim to avoid "the myth of coherence"[9], if I correctly understand that to be beguiled by the myth is to try to impose a false unity on the thought of a given writer. It is certainly not part of my thesis to deny there are any strains, tensions or conflicts in Mill's liberalism. Indeed, I shall draw attention to what seem to be the most important of these even while arguing that certain alleged fundamental inconsistencies are not really such. But what I shall chiefly seek to show is that Mill may fairly be described as a liberal. He is a liberal because of his genuine and encompassing concern for individual liberty and because the tensions in his theory normally arise out of what he saw as the main problem for his liberalism: The problem of showing how the autonomy and diversity which he treasured so much could be provided for within the confines of a sustaining yet non-oppressive moral and social community. The side of this problem which concerned Mill most was that of securing the development of liberty, individuality and self-perfection in the face of the increasingly conformist social morality of the newly emerging social democracies. His principle of self-protection was designed to protect individuals from social coercion and so provide them with spheres of activity within which they could freely pursue their ideals of self-perfection. There is, however, another side to Mill's liberalism. The operation of the sanctions allowed by the principle of self-protection was not in itself enough to ensure a condition of equal freedom and happiness for all. It was also necessary, Mill believed, for the members of a society to be positively altruistic, to associate the attainment of their own freedom and happiness with that of every other member of the community and, ultimately, with that of all of humanity. Altruism as a principle of action would be inculcated by means of education. Such education would, of necessity, be the prerogative of the wisest and most developed members of the community, though Mill rejected Comte's scheme for its being carried out by an elite organised in a corporate hierarchy.

---

[9] See Quentin Skinner "Political Theory: The Unimportance of the Great Texts", A paper read to the Political Studies Association Conference, 1968.

Mill's general problem, in both of its sides, is necessarily endemic to liberalism. How is it possible to formulate and embody in appropriate institutions a practical philosophy of politcs which will give the freest scope to the pursuit of a variety of ideals and yet have due regard for the general welfare? A number of the most characteristic tensions in Mill's liberalism arise out of his efforts to grapple with various aspects of this recurring problem. Hence the charges of inconsistency and of illiberalism. Hence, too, the continued relevance for us of much of what Mill had to say.

Moral Individualism in a Transitional Age

Let us now turn to a preliminary consideration of the concept or vision of man which underlies Mill's liberalism. Mill is a moral individualist in the very broadest sense, in taking the conception of a good individual as the cornerstone of his ethics and in assuming that the goodness of all other things must be derived from that notion. If the notion of the good man is at the foundation of his moral doctrine then what is it that makes a man good? According to Mill, it is primarily his power of thinking and acting for himself and in so doing developing his higher capacities. The highest good is individuality or self-determination, conceived of as the chief condition of and the main ingredient in the life of self-development. Mill is a classic moral individualist in regarding as the highest human excellence the individual's capacity for making rational choices among competing views and ways of life and striving to be true to his sense of dignity. Mill possesses a deep and unshakeable attachment to the dignity and responsibility of the individual human being and to his having a presumptive right to decide for himself what is to be morally binding upon him. This is just to say that Mill, like Kant, is deeply committed to treating individuals as ends in themselves. Mill's view is that an action's being good is essentially linked to the fact that it is freely chosen, so that if individuals are to attain the good life others must respect their right to pursue their own ideals in their own way. A corollary of this doctrine of respect for indivduals is that men and women should be free to do as they like unless some good reason can be found for restricitng their activities. Mill himself believed that the only allowable reason for interfering with the freedom of adult, civilized individuals was to prevent their damaging the interests of others.

Now, the concept of individuality involved in classic moral individualism is embodied in and partly constitutive of a particular form of society. The form of society in question has not always existed and is usually thought to have had its beginnings in Europe during the fourteenth and fifteenth centuries. In previous, traditional societies like that of the closely integrated life of the Greek polis or of the feudal communities, the social conditions in which individuality could emerge were, for most men, absent. In such societies a man defined himself, and his identity was fixed, in terms of a limited set of clearly defined social roles and functions. Those societies were hostile to the growth of any high degree of human individuality: though a man in such a society was an indivual in the sense of being a separate biological and physical being, his conception of himself was largely determined by the norms of his own particular social group. His condition has recently been described by Michael Oakeshott:

> "To know oneself as the member of a family, a group, a corporation, a church, a village community, as the suitor at a court or as the occupier of a tenancy, has been for the vast majority, the circumstantially possible sum of self-knowledge."[10]

Anyone brought up in this type of society is bound (if I may borrow Mill's words out of context), to let "the world choose his plan of life for him", since his group is the only 'world' he knows and it assigns to him his station and the path he must follow through life. Because his path in life is laid out for him, his opportunities for choice are narrowly circumscribed and he becomes so dependent on the norms and traditions of his group that he never grows accustomed to making his own choices, to asserting himself continuously and independently, to pursuing his own lines of activity.

In such societies there was no unbridgeable gulf between fact and value. For the member of such a society his fundamental moral evaluations are laid down for him by his social role. From the fact that he occupies a certain preordained place in the social order (specified in terms of his status, class or family) it follows ineluctably he has certain duties or

---

[10] M. Oakeshott, "The Masses in Representative Democracy", in A.H. Hunold (ed.) *Freedom and Serfdom* (Holland, 1961) p.152.

obligations to fulfil. Thus in specifying his status in the social structure we are necessarily ascribing to him certain duties or obligations.

The gradual breakdown of medieval society in Europe set in motion a vast historical process which brought into being a new form of society, one favourable to the growth and extension of individuality. The process brought in its train a profound change in the relationship between the individual and the social groups to which he belonged; he was no longer immoveably tied to one or two groups - an extended family, a church, a village community, a manor, a guild. Associated with the beginnings of individualist society was the social movement and doctrine of moral individualism, which became the cornerstone of European liberalism. When liberalism is spoken of as being individualistic, at "the heart of what is meant", as Charles Frankel has put it, is the "drive to release the individual from unalterable dependence on any particular social group".[11] Implicit in the denial that a man's identity is established simply by his functional roles in family, church, guild and so on, was an entirely new concept of man. This was the concept of man as an *individual*, as an autonomous moral agent, endowed with the capacity of self-determination, capable of pursuing his own good in his own way. In Frankel's words, it was "the concept of the free, mobile individual, moving around from place to place, moving up or down in society as he had the chance, and retaining, as the one continuing thread of personal identity, his judging mind, his feeling heart, his personal conscience. . ."[12] Thus the individual no longer finds his moral commitments largely made for him in terms of a very limited number of fixed social roles. In an individualist society man becomes conscious of himself as a person and can begin to ask himself such questions as 'How shall I live?' 'What is the best life for me?' His identity has become personal: instead of being in large measure simply the bearer of a few well-defined social roles carrying fixed responsibilities he is more and more obliged to make up his own mind in the face of the competing attractions of alternative opinions and differing ways of life.

---

[11] Charles Frankel, *The Case for Modern Man* (New York, 1955) p.31.
[12] Charles Frankel, "The Awful Idea of Being an Individual" in *The Love of Anxiety* (New York, 1965) p.111.

The classical individualist concept of man was, then, actually embodied in and partially constitutive of, the new form of social life then emerging in Western Europe. Those who had escaped or were escaping from the communal pressures of family, church and so forth *were* individuals; they were accustomed to thinking for themselves and expressing their own preferences and they *thought of themselves* and those resembling themselves as having individual character. What this serves to bring out is that the doctrine of moral individualism carries with it its own concept of human nature and that concept was in part instantiated in the newly emerging individualist society. Liberal individualism pictures man as a being who is most himself when he is exercising his capacity for free choice, when he chooses his own moral criteria and when what he thinks or does on any particular occasion is the product of his own unique personality. And this picture of human nature is not arbitrarily adopted by the exponent of liberal individualism. For in adopting the individualist mode of life he *ipso facto* subscribes to an individualist concept of man; the individualist form of life or society and the individualist concept of man are inextricably bound up together.

Mill believed that in his own day Western European society was coming to the end of its individualist or "critical" phase. For this reason he thought of the earlier, "negative" liberalism of the Benthamites as having done its best work and as in crucial respects no longer relevant to the problems of the coming post-individualist or "organic" age. Hence he came to see his chief purpose as that of reformulating the liberal-utilitarianism he had inherited from Bentham and his father. He saw his main mission as that of fashioning a new 'positive' and humanistic liberalism which would assist his era in making the long transition to a new state of society. Such a society, he hoped, would be a "critical-organic society": it would combine the best elements of individualist society with the best elements of a Greek city-state or feudal society. The new liberal-progressive society would be a pluralistic society of autonomous individuals each striving to realize his own personal ideals within the framework of a common social morality. Social and political institutions would be so designed as to provide for individual and social diversity while enabling men and women to strengthen their capacity for judgment and responsible choice and to deepen their interest in the general welfare by participating with others in the management of the common affairs of the society. The guiding purpose of the state would be to promote the public interest by maintaining a system of sanctions designed to uphold the principles of justice. The specific functions of the state would ultimately be under the control of the people; the government would be a representative democracy. At the same time a moral and social consensus, an altruistic "Religion of Humanity", would be formulated and promulgated by an openly recruited moral and intellectual elite. The Religion of Humanity is designed to reinforce by *persuasive* means the coercive controls of government and society. The function of social and political leaders is to help people develop their individuality and to try to ensure that in so doing each individual may learn to associate the attainment of his own self-development with the happiness and development of all other members of the community. The attitude of the majority to the leadership would be one of critical deference; and in carrying out their programme of reform liberal leaders would eschew coercion, would rely entirely on education or persuasion.

The Function of Social Philosophy

For Mill, then, social philosophy was a normative activity: it was an attempt to reformulate Benthamite liberalism in such a way as to provide a comprehensive and realistic strategy for the transition of his own 'critical' age to a new critical-organic society. Looking back upon this project now it is impossible for us to share the optimism implied in Mill's view of his own mission. Yet we must not forget that his intellectual and moral optimism was shared by many social thinkers and philosophers of history of the nineteenth century. Behind such optimism lies a belief in the power of ideas to influence and even markedly to alter the direction of the course of social change. Mill thought that by formulating and propagating a social philosophy of liberal humanism, which would retain the best in Benthamite liberalism and be an alternative to existing moral and political views, he might so influence educated opinion as to be able to redirect the course of social and political change.

Mill's confidence in the social influence of moral speculation and teaching springs from his conviction that ideology is the driving force of history. "It is what men think that determines how they act".[13] Or again, "there really is one social element which is thus predominant, and almost paramount, among the agents of the social progression. This is the state of the speculative faculties of mankind, including the nature of the beliefs which by any means they have arrived at concerning themselves and the world by which they are surrounded".[14] These words express a principal tenet of Mill's philosophy of history. Conservatism, Marxism, linguistic philosophy and sociology are among the intellectual influences which have led to some loss of confidence in the power of a body of ideals to shape the direction of large-scale social change. Certainly we are now more aware of the extent to which a political philosophy arises out of or comes to be formulated in connection with social activities and ways of life. But an examination of Mill's views of the role of social philosophy in social change would require an extended discussion of Mill's philosophy of history. Here I have space enough only for two brief observations. First, the link between moral and political principles may be more, or less, intimate; as a matter of history it has *not always* been the case that an ideology has been as Oakeshott has expressed it, the mere "abridgement" of a prevailing social practice. Secondly (and this point is of more relevance to my thesis), it is extremely doubtful whether it is wise or even possible to dispense with the guiding function of a social philosophy in human affairs. Speculative extrapolation of social trends currently observable, moral and political evaluation of various current forms of human activity and of their putative future outcomes, such assessments are surely both vital and inescapable in the life of a sophisticated society. In making out a case for a liberal social philosophy Charles Frankel has described a "social philosophy" or "philosophy of history" in this way:

> "A philosophy of history offers us a long view and a hard view. It gives us a chance to keep first things first, and lifts political action above the level of expediency and opportunism. For the attempt to develop a philosophy of history has been a way in which men have tried to make a sober and circumspect appraisal of the historical resources available to them, the limits upon their powers, and the alternatives open to them. It has been an attempt to deal with problems, not in isolation from one another but in some systematic way, to take account of long-range considerations, to safeguard primary ideals, to pick out

---

[13] Mill, *Representative Government* (Everyman edition) p.184. Hereafter the abbreviation 'RG' will be used for all references to this work.
[14] J.S. Mill, *A System of Logic* (London, 1949, 8th Edition) p.604.

the most important variables in the social process. A philosophy of history can be a way, at once, of making the social imagination more responsible by pinning it down to what is immovable, and of making it free and more flexible by giving it a larger vision of human possibilities. It is a theory of how things get done in history and of what men can make of their history. As such, it is an important strategy of social action, and it can be a sober prelude to the development of a coherent social programme".[15]

Frankel is right to point out that unless liberal-democratic politics is to be reduced to an unfocussed, bread-and-butter affair of bargaining between parties and factions it requires ideas, ideas concerning what are the enduring ideals of human excellence, reasonably determinate pictures of better forms of society and realistic strategies for their attainment.

The Three 'Levels' of Mill's Liberalism

A philosophy of history closely matching Frankel's specifications lies below the particular values and concrete social and political programmes which go to make up the 'surface' or 'superstructure' of Mill's liberalism. Mill's liberalism, as I shall show, is a fairly coherent body of ideas in which it is possible to distinguish three differentiable but interconnected types or 'levels' of thinking and argument.[16] The first is what may be called the philosophical level. A social and political philosophy will embody a web of theory and argument concerned with the analysis and justification of general logical, metaphysical and epistemological principles. It will that is to say, attempt to support conclusions concerning both particular moral and social values and particular social and political institutions by linking those conclusions with more general theories concerning the logical structure of the world; the foundation of knowledge; the nature of man. Secondly, connected with these very general beliefs and 'supported' by them will be a set of more concrete moral and social values: particular liberties; various

---

[15] Charles Frankel, *The Case for Modern Man, op. cit.,* p.7.
[16] The following sketch of the various "levels" of thinking in social philsophy owes much to the discussion of this question by P.H. Partridge in *Thinking About Politics* (Canberra, 1956); "Politics, Philosophy, Ideology", *Political Studies*, vol.9, 1961; and "Political Philosophy and Political Sociology", *The Australian and New Zealand Journal of Sociology*, vol.1, April, 1965. See also Bernard Williams, "Democracy and Ideology", *The Political Quarterly*, vol.32, 1961.

types of equality; justice, authority and so forth. The social philosopher is concerned moreover, not simply with the clarification and analysis of such values but also with their criticism and reformulation in the light of changing human needs and altered social circumstances. What is more, this second level of political thinking is a two-way process: "it is the process of amending and extending our conceptions in the light of changing needs and circumstances, while, at the same time, criticising and judging circumstances in the light of principles".[17] It follows that if the second level of thinking is not to be utterly Utopian, it will have to contain a good deal of sociological generalization. For this reason we find embedded in much social philosophy speculative sociological theories and theories of history - theories about social necessities and about the possibilities of social development or change. At the third and final level, a social or political philosophy will contain a more or less detailed account of the specific social and political arrangements or institutions within and by which the good life is to be realized; this account will, in particular, normally include some discussion of the proper purposes or functions of the state.

Mill's liberalism exemplifies reasonably clearly the tripartite structure of a social philosophy and as we proceed I shall endeavour to trace the most important of the relationships between the three parts of that structure.

---

[17] P.H. Partridge, *Thinking About Politics*, op.cit., p.20.

CHAPTER II

UTILITY AND MORAL INDIVIDUALISM

Happiness and Self-Development

Mill believed it indispensable to connect his social philosophy with a theory concerning the nature of things in general, the foundations of knowledge and the nature of man. Man himself is seen as part of a single natural order, subject to explanation and examination by the scientific method; and a social philosophy is seen as in certain important respects linked to a comprehensive doctrine of nature and human nature. Nor had Mill any doubt that his social philosophy could be firmly grounded upon an empiricist logic and epistemology. I propose now to indicate how Mill considers social philsophy to be related to his empiricist theory of mind.

I have already observed that behind the body of particular principles and concrete programmes which make up the substance of a social philosophy there will be a more or less explicit conception of man. It will be a conception of man's essential needs or potentialities, of what he characteristically is and, even more, what he is at his best. The fundmental moral and psychological idea upon which Mill's liberalism rests is his view of man as a being capable of self-determination and independent judgment, a being who reveals his distinctive excellence in this mode of activity. I turn now to a further explication of his conception of the good life for man.

Stated in a few words, the psychological and moral doctrine underlying Mill's liberalism is that man differs from animals primarily in possessing certain special endowments - the intellectual, moral, emotional and aesthetic capacities - and that the highest possible development of these capacities makes for the best and happiest life. Whilst it is most fully and consistently elaborated in the *Liberty*, the doctrine that the chief end for man is "self-development" also emerges (even if rather confusedly) in *Utilitarianism;* it is further referred to in the *Autobiography* and there are distinct traces of it to be found in the *Logic,* in the *Principles of Political Economy* and in a number of the shorter essays, especially the essay on Bentham. Of course, Mill is customarily thought of as a utilitarian, but the truth is that he does not have an unequivocal view of the nature of the good life. Throughout his writings he continued to profess that the general happiness is the ultimate end, but he believed also that one could not be a ultilitarian without being an individualist and conceived of self-development as the prime constituent of happiness.

Writing to Carlyle in 1834 Mill said he was and was likely to remain a utilitarian, "though not one of 'the people called utilitarians'; indeed, having scarcely one of my secondary premises in common with them".[1] Mill's modified view first emerged in his "Remarks on Bentham's Philosophy", published anonymously in 1833. His revision of Benthamism was continued in "Professor Sedgwick's Discourse on the Studies of the University of Cambridge" (1835)' "Bentham" (1838); and "Coleridge" (1840). Later in life Mill endeavoured to play down his departures from orthodox Benthamism, notably in *Utilitarianism;* but even there, as we shall see, the differences remain substantial.

A great deal has been written concerning the various respects in which Mill attempts to reformulate Benthamite Utilitarianism, and in certain respects Mill's reformulations are notoriously obscure. Since my thesis is an examination of Mill's liberalism and not of his utilitarianism I am entitled to put aside some of the difficult questions of interpretation which arise in this area. For instance, I shall not canvass the vexed problem as to whether Mill is properly considered an act or a rule-utilitarian. Because of their relevance for the concept of human nature underlying his liberalism it is, however, essential for me to examine those elements of Mill's moral psychology which taken together constitute a notable departure from the orthodox Benthamite picture of man.

Mill says that the first question we must ask of any philosopher is, "what is his theory of life?"[2] He observes that in the case of Bentham "there were large deficiencies and hiatuses in his scheme of human nature and

---

[1] F. Mineka (ed.) *The Earlier Letters of John Stuart Mill,* vol.XII, (Toronto, 1963) Letter 95, p.207.
[2] "Bentham", in Himmelfarb, *op.cit.,* p.96.

life and a consequent want of breadth and comprehension in his secondary principles."[3]   Mill's general objection to Bentham's political thought was that it rested upon a crude psychological hedonism since it attempted to explain human action simply in terms of self-interest. According to Mill, Bentham failed to see that disinterested motives, though not originally part of a man's endowment, could be acquired by him through the association of ideas. In terms of this explanation, Mill adds to the list of independent human motives attributed to men by Bentham and thus builds up a more adequate view of human nature and hence of the good life for men.

Mill's revision of orthodox utilitarian moral psychology has several related aspects. All stem from Mill's quite general criticism that Benthamism failed to appreciate that cultivating individual character is at the centre of the good life. First I address myself to an appraisal of this general critique. Three specific inter-related objections issuing from the general critique will then be considered in turn. They are: (1) Mill's rejection of Bentham's view that men always act for the sake of obtaining *future* pleasures or avoiding *future* pains; (2) his criticism of Bentham's failure to include among the relevant consequences of an action its effect on the agent's own character; (3) Mill's well-known revision of the Benthamite notion of "pleasure".[4] Of these, (2) and (3) are the most radical of Mill's modifications of strict Benthamite hedonistic utilitarianism and have the most far-reaching implications for Mill's liberalism.

Morality and Individual Character

Looking back upon the consequences of his mental crisis, Mill says it led to two major changes in his opinions and character. The first of these will be discussed shortly. The second is introduced by Mill's recalling "that I, for the first time, gave its proper place, among the prime necessities of human well-being, to the internal culture of the individual. I ceased to attach almost exclusive importance to the ordering of outward circumstances, and the training of the human being for speculation and for

---

[3] "Dr. Whewell on Moral Philosophy", in Schneewind (ed.) *Mill's Ethical Writings, op.cit.,* p.179.
[4] Discussion of (3) will be deferred until Chapter IV.

action".[5] The chief deficiency of Benthamite ethics, Mill is intimating, was its one-sided concentration on outward circumstances to the neglect of individual character, more especially the emotional and aesthetic side of human character. Mill's reaction against Benthamism now led him to place particular stress upon the cultivation of the feelings and imagination as part of the good life. He discovered that "the passive susceptibilities need to be cultivated as well as the active capacities" and whilst he did not thereby depreciate the value of intellectual activity and practical action he came to see the need for balance in the good life: "The maintenance of a due balance among the faculties, now seemed to me of primary importance. The cultivation of the feelings became one of the cardinal points in my ethical and philosophical creed".[6] Poetry and the arts of drama, music and painting, Mill had begun to realise, are not only perennial sources of delight and a vital ingredient of individual happiness but also "instruments of human culture," being of "value as aids in the formation of character".[7] He came to see as well that it was not merely the aesthetic feelings which might best be developed through the use of the imagination, the reading of poetry, the enjoyment of music and the appreciation of the beauty of nature, From poetry and from history too, one could obtain sustenance for the sympathetic feelings and acquire a much greater interest in "the common feelings and common destiny of human beings".[8] Mill is here linking the development of altruism with the "cultivation of the feelings"; in the enjoyment of art we come through the exercise of the imagination, to enter into and appreciate the feelings and circumstances of our fellow human beings.[9] The artist helps us to participate in the mental states and emotions of others, he develops our capacity for sympathy; and only on this foundation is it possible to build up a genuine or disinterested morality.

---

[5] *Autobiography* (New York: Columbia University Press, 1924) p.100.
[6] *Ibid.,* p.101.
[7] *Ibid.,* pp.101, 106. Mill aimed, as he says, to "soften the harder and sterner features" of eighteenth century radicalism and utilitarianism and to provide "a utilitarianism which takes into account the whole of human nature", a utilitarianism in which feeling would be as valuable as thought and poetry "the necessary condition of any true and comprehensive Philosophy." Letter to Edward Lytton Bulwer, 23rd November, 1836. F. Mineka (ed.) *The Earlier Letters of John Stuart Mill, op.cit.,* vol.XII, Letter 181, p.312.
[8] *Autobiography, op.cit.,* pp.101-4 and cf. *Utilitarianism* (Everyman ed.) p.13.
[9] "Bentham" in Himmelfarb, *op.cit.,* p.94.

We here see Mill struggling to take account of a side of life and morality grossly neglected by earlier Benthamite liberals. What this side of morality may be is further suggested in a letter to John Sterling. "The *spirit* of all morality," Mill wrote, is "right self-culture, the principles of which cannot change, since man's nature changes not, though surrounding circumstances do. . . all I mean is that it is culture of the man's self, of his feelings and will, fitting him to look abroad and see how he is to act, not imposing upon him by express definition, a prescribed mode of action."[10] Mill is here presaging an individualist conception of morality whose implications for his liberalism are far-reaching, as he was later to make much more explicit. His view is that the "*spirit* of all morality" is "self-culture"; or, as he puts it in "Bentham", the "moral part of man's nature in the *strict* sense of the term", is "the desire of perfection, or the feeling of an approving or of an accusing conscience".[11] Because Bentham's theory of morality rests on a conception of man as being governed mainly by self-interest and never by the desire for "spiritual perfection", it cannot even "pretend to aid individuals in the formation of their own character". Bentham never came to recognise man "as being capable of pursuing spiritual perfection as an end; of desiring, for its own sake, the conformity of his own character to his standard of excellence, without hope of good or fear of evil from other sources than his own inward conscience". Bentham only faintly acknowledges, as part of human psychology, the pursuit of such other ideal ends as "the sense of *honour*, and personal dignity"; the love of beauty and of order and the love of power, in the sense of "the power of making our volitions effectual; the love of action, the thirst for movement and activity. . . ." In short, Bentham's ethics does not recognise in human nature the "power" or "wish" for "self-culture" and so can do little to aid the promotion of that "grand duty of man".[12]

---

[10] Letter to John Sterling, 24th May, 1832. F. Mineka (ed.) *The Earlier Letters of John Stuart Mill, op.cit.,* Vol.XII, Letter 50, p.101. Italics in original. The influence of Coleridge may well have been at work here. The philosophers of the Germano-Coleridgian school, according to Mill, "looked upon the culture of the inward man as the problem of problems". "Coleridge", in Himmelfarb, *op.cit.,* p.145.
[11] "Bentham", in Himmelfarb, *op.cit.,* p.98. My emphasis.
[12] The several preceding passages from "Bentham" are in Himmelfarb, pp.97-100. Italics in original.

In these passages it is evident Mill is moving away from the simple psychological hedonism of Bentham towards a more sophisticated and realistic moral psychology. Orthodox utilitarianism was for him an altogether too barren creed, since it failed to point up the fact that in order for man to achieve the deepest sort of happiness it was necessary for him to fulfil his moral and spiritual needs or potentialities. Mill came to see that Bentham had been altogether too shallow in supposing that what men need to make them really happy is no more than to satisfy as many of their desires as possible, irrespective of the nature of those desires. He became aware that men and women are - or may, if given the opportunity, become - not just beings bent upon satisfying a train of desires (for food, drink, sex, bodily comfort and so forth) but also creatures with a sense of "dignity" or "self-respect", who aspire to make themselves worthy of the consideration of others and who strive in some degree to call forth their nobler feelings and capacities, and to be what they believe it is proper for them to be.

Morality and Consequences

As Mill reveals in his *Autobiography,* the harrowing experience of his mental crisis led him gradually to reconsider the orthodox Benthamite account of human motivation. Though he still believed happiness to be "the test of all rules of conduct, and the end of life" he came to think happiness could only be attained by not making it a direct or conscious goal; rather, by aiming at "ideal" or secondary ends other than happiness we find happiness by the way.[13] The import of this counsel for Mill's rethinking of Benthamism emerges more clearly in his "Remarks on Bentham's Philosophy", where he is correcting what he considers to be one of the more serious distortions in Bentham's formulation of the doctrine of psychological egoism. He is there complaining that Bentham's misunderstanding of the role of consequences in human activity leads to a seriously misleading conception of human motivation. Bentham's psychological hedonism involves the unwarranted assumption "that all our acts are determined by pains and pleasures *in prospect,* pains and pleasures to which we look forward as the *consequences* of our acts".[14]

---

[13] *Autobiography, op.cit.,* p.100.
[14] "Remarks on Bentham's Philosophy" in J.B. Schneewind, *Mill's Ethical Writings, op.cit.,* p.55. Italics in original.

What Bentham fails to observe, is that our conduct is generally determined by our *present* idea of the pleasantness or pain of the act, not by our further idea of its consequences.

As against Bentham, Mill's own psychological theory allows that we may act in acccordance with the pleasantness or unpleasantness of our *present* states of mind without calculating what future pleasures and pains are likely to result from our acts. Benthamite hedonism cannot account for disinterested or virtuous actions, which it converts into mere means for the attainment of pleasure, the single, external end. Mill's view is rather that because we come to associate them with what they regularly lead to, we can come to regard certain actions and states of character simply as pleasant in themselves. What once were valued as means only now become constituents in happiness in that they are desired in and for themselves and not for their external consequences. Virtue, for instance, being once merely a means to pleasure or avoidance of pain, has come, "through the association thus formed" to be felt as a good in itself, as an important part of or ingredient in happiness.[15]

In thus introducing into his theory the notion that dispositions and activities may be inherently pleasant, Mill tacitly abandons hedonistic utilitarianism. He may, though, be confronted with the following dilemma. If it is the pleasure associated with being virtuous which confers intrinsic value on a virtuous action, then it is pleasure, not virtue, which is intrinsically good. If, on the other hand, it is the virtuous activity that is good in itself, no matter how pleasant or unpleasant it is felt to be, then pleasure is no longer the sole intrinsic good.

The Two Parts of Morality

When Mill wrote to Sterling that the "*spirit* of all morality" is "right self-culture" he was hinting at a view of morality which he develops (in the course of a critique of Bentham) in his "Remarks on Bentham's Philosophy" and in his essays on Bentham and Sedgwick. The importance of this conception of morality for an understanding of Mill's liberalism has received

---

[15] *Utilitarianism* (Everyman edition, 1910), p.35. All future references to this work are indicated by the abbreviation 'U'.

too little attention. Indeed the writings in which this aspect of his ethical theory is set down have themselves been largely neglected.[16] The part played by this concept of morality in Mill's theory of moral progress will be commented upon shortly. In the meantime I confine myself to further exploration of Mill's revision of the earlier utilitarian conception of morality.

A central objection Mill makes to Bentham's moral theory is that he fails to include among the relevant consequences of an action its effect on the agent's own state of mind and its relation to the formation of his character. One of Bentham's worst faults as a moral philosopher was his assuming that the rightness or wrongness of an action is to be assessed in terms of its "specific consequences". Mill writes:

> "He [Bentham] has largely exemplified, and contributed very widely to diffuse, a tone of thinking according to which any kind of action or any habit, which in its own specific consequences cannot be proved to be necessarily or probably productive of unhappiness to the agent himself or to others, is supposed to be fully justified; and any disapprobation or aversion entertained towards the individual by reason of it, is set down from that time forward as prejudice and superstition. It is not considered (at least, not habitually considered), whether the act or habit in question, though not in itself pernicious, may not form part of a character essentially pernicious, or at least essentially deficient in some quality eminently conducive to the "greatest happiness". To apply such a standard as this, would indeed often require a much deeper insight into the formation of character, and knowledge of the internal working of human nature, than Mr. Bentham possessed. But, in a greater or less degree, he, and every one else, judges by this standard". [17]

The "consequence" left out of account by Bentham is the effect of an action on the character of the agent. In Mill's view, this is always a critical aspect of moral judgment and one, moreover, which is embedded in the common moral consciousness. Nonetheless, when they came to discuss particular ethical questions Bentham and many of his followers "have commonly, in the superior stress which they laid upon the specific consequences of a

---

[16] This hitherto neglected aspect of Mill's moral theory has recently been singled out for some attention by Maurice Mandelbaum in "On Interpreting Mill's Utilitarianism", *Journal of the History of Philosophy,* Vo.VI, No.1, January, 1968. See also R.J. Halliday, "Some Recent Interpretations of John Stuart Mill", *Philosophy,* Vol.XLIII, No.163, January, 1968.
[17] "Remarks on Bentham's Philsophy", *op.cit.,* pp.49-50. Italics in original. Quoted by Mandelbaum, *op.cit.,* p.41.

class of acts, rejected all contemplation of the action in its general bearings upon the entire moral being of the agent".[18]

Mill argues that certain types of action, for example, thieving or lying would, if generally practised, bring about evil social consequences. But such consequences are not the only relevant consideration when we are judging the morality of such actions. "All acts suppose certain dispositions and habits of mind and heart, which may be in themselves states of enjoyment or wretchedness, and which must be fruitful in other consequences besides those particular acts. No person can be a thief or a liar without being much else, and if our moral judgments and feelings with respect to a person convicted of either vice were grounded solely upon the pernicious tendency of thieving and lying, they would be partial and incomplete".[19] In thus failing to take sufficiently into account "the relation of an act to a certain state of mind as its cause", Bentham revealed himself unable fully to appreciate the influence of habit on the formation of character. "For it may be affirmed with few exceptions, that any act whatever has a tendency to fix and perpetuate the state or character of mind in which itself has originated."[20] Hence among the less obvious but most significant effects of actions (both good and bad) are those which, through force of habit, come to have a deep and long-term influence on the feeling and character of the agent.

That this view of morality is a considered one, not an isolated doctrine confined to Mill's anonymous essay on Bentham, is confirmed when one turns to the article on Sedgwick and to the published essay on Bentham. In the article on Sedgwick, in a key passage, he writes:

> "In estimating the consequences of actions, in order to obtain a measure of their morality, there are always two sets of considerations involved: the consequences to the outward interests of the parties concerned (including the agent himself), and the consequences to the characters of the same persons, and to their outward interests so far as dependent upon their characters. In the estimation of the first of these two classes of considerations, there is in general not much difficulty, nor much room for difference of opinion. The actions which are directly hurtful, or directly useful, to the outward interests of oneself or of

---
[18] *Ibid.*, p.49. Italics in original.
[19] *Ibid.*, p.49. Italics in original.
[20] *Ibid.*, p.50.

> other people, are easily distinguished, sufficiently at least for the guidance of a private individual. The rights of individuals, which other individuals ought to respect, over external things, are in general sufficiently pointed out by a few plain rules, and by the laws of one's country. But it often happens that an essential part of the morality or immorality of an action or a rule of action consists in its influence upon the agent's own mind: upon his susceptibilities of pleasure or pain, upon the general direction of his thoughts, feelings, and imagination, or upon some particular association."[21]

Mill here explicitly introduces the doctrine, adumbrated earlier, that morality consists of two parts or involves "two sets of considerations": those relating to "outward interests" and those concerning the individual character. This distinction differentiates Mill's view sharply from Bentham's and has deep implications for Mill's views on social reform and on the scope and limits of liberty. It is taken up again and more fully expounded in the later essay on Bentham.

"Morality", Mill there states, "consists of two parts. One of these is self-education; the training, by the human being himself, of his affections and will. That department is a blank in Bentham's system. The other and coequal part, the regulation of his outward actions, must be altogether halting and imperfect without the first: for how can we judge in what manner many an action will affect the worldly interests of ourselves or others, unless we take in, as part of the question, its influence on the regulation of our, or their, affections and desires?"[22] On a strict Benthamite view, the rightness or wrongness of an action is to be assessed in terms of its outward consequences. Mill now says that on the contrary morality is or should be concerned not merely with the external consequences of actions but also with the cultivation of certain dispositions or traits of character. In judging whether an action is right or wrong we have to consider its effect on the development and perfection of the *character* of the agent and those affected as well as on his and their "worldly interests". Mill even, as we noted, goes so far as to say that "the spirit of all morality" is "right self-culture"; and that the "moral part of man's nature in the strict sense of the term" is "the desire of perfection, or the feeling of an approving or

---

[21] "Professor Sedgwick's Discourse on the Studies of the University of Cambridge", in Schneewind, *op.cit.*, p.84. Quoted in part by M. Mandelbaum, *op.cit.*, p.41.
[22] "Bentham", in Himmelfarb *op.cit.*, p.100.

accusing conscience". And he castigates Bentham for relying on a practical philosophy of life which takes no account of "moral influences".[23] It is by no means clear how one should interpret these statements. Are we to undersand Mill as here relinquishing his view of morality as having two different and "co-equal" parts? Mill now seems to be subscribing to two different, incompatible views of morality: (1) The dual aspect theory, according to which morality has two co-equal parts, the one concerned with self-education, the other with outward interests; (2) The view that, in the "spiritual" or "strict" sense, morality is concerned simply with self-culture. Perhaps these passages are to be regarded as symptoms of the phase of strong reaction against Benthamite orthodoxy Mill was going through at the time? My view of the matter is that these dicta should not be taken to commit Mill to relinquishing the view that outward consequences are relevant in moral judgment. Rather, what he seems most concerned to stress is that the spiritual aspect of morality so neglected by Bentham is really the most important side of morality. This suggests that he is more deeply committed not to a morality of "co-equal" parts but to a dual aspect theory of morality in which the spiritual aspect is seen to be of greater importance. As we shall see in a later chapter, however, he was soon to abandon this theory in favour of the view that "self-education" is, strictly speaking, aesthetic or noble rather than moral.

Morality and Legislation

Bentham's inadequate moral psychology with its resulting one-sided conception of morality led in Mill's view to a serious flaw in Benthamite social and political philosophy. According to Bentham, each man acts to achieve what he takes to be his greatest personal good or interest. Hence Bentham's conception of society is "of a collection of persons pursuing each his separate interest or pleasure."[24] The function of the legislator is, by means of what Bentham called the "Duty-and-Interest-Juncture-Producing principle", to prevent individuals from jostling one another unduly and so make personal interest and common interest coincide. This coincidence could be brought about, Bentham supposed, by an elaborate system of political, religious and popular, external sanctions. The sanctions

---

[23] *Ibid.,* p.102.
[24] "Bentham", *op.cit.,* p.100.

would be so ordered as to attach pleasurable rewards to beneficial actions and painful penalties to harmful ones. A nice balance of such sanctions would so arrange matters that each perosn would be so motivated that in gratifying his own desires he would be led to act in such a way as *ipso facto* to do what is in the interest of all.

Mill was willing to grant that this ethical theory of Bentham's was adequate as a philosophy of legislation. "It can teach the means of organising and regulating the merely *business* part of the social arrangements. Whatever can be understood or whatever done without moral influences, his philosophy is equal to."[25] The legislator characteristically exercises his authority by means of a system of commands or prohibitions and enforces them by means of a set of rewards and punishments. By these means he can only hope to regulate adequately the "outward" actions of citizens. "The legislator," in Mill's view, "enjoins or prohibits an action, with very little regard to the general moral excellence or turpitude which it implies; he looks to the consequences to society of the particular kind of action; his object is not to render people incapable of *desiring* a crime, but to deter them from actually *committing* it."[26] The function of the legislator is not to attempt to influence our moral dispositions. Rather, by the employment of sanctions he prevents our engaging in activities like murder, arson and theft, which are manifestly harmful to others. The role of the legislator is to formulate and enforce a body of legal rules by which a society is able to "protect its material interests."

Whether or not Mill sees this as a 'moral' function depends on which of his definitions of morality is applied. If (as he sometimes maintains) morality includes, as one of its "coequal" parts, the regulation of the business side of life, then the state does have a moral function. But if, as he elsewhere has it, morality is essentially concerned with self-culture, then the state can have no direct role to play in the moral life.

While at one level Bentham's doctrine concerning legislation was adequate for dealing with the outward details of legislation, at a deeper level it was, Mill thought, insufficient even for that purpose. The legislator is

---

[25] *Ibid.*, p.102. Italics in original.
[26] "Remarks on Bentham's Philosophy," *op.cit.*, p.51. Italics in original.

concerned with preventing acts that bring evil consequences and promoting those that bring good consequences. There is, though, an intimate connection between acts, habit and individual character in that all acts, if repeated, tend to "fix and perpetuate the state of character or mind" in which they originate. For this reason, material or outward interests of a society themselves depend upon the character of the citizens. "That which alone causes any material interests to exist, which alone enables any body of human beings to exist as a society, is national character. . . The true teacher of the fitting social arrangements for England, France, or America, is the one who can point out how the English, French or American character can be improved, and how it has been made what it is. A philosophy of laws and institutions, not founded on a philosophy of national character is an absurdity."[27] Mill wishes to argue that material interests depend upon personal character and that personal character in turn is closely connected with the social and policial institutions of society. The main deficiency of Bentham's political philosophy is that since he failed to see the connection between acts and character he was unable to appreciate the powerful influence of social education on character. "It never seems to have occurred to him to regard political institutions in a higher light, as the principal means of the social education of a people."[28] A political philosophy such as Bentham's "will be most apt to fail in the consideration of the greater social question: the theory of organic institutions and general forms of policy; for these (unlike the details of legislation) to be duly estimated, must be viewed as the great instruments of forming the national character, of carrying forward the members of the community towards perfection, or preserving them from degeneracy."[29] In summary, Mill's charge is that nowhere had Benthamite liberalism been so deficient as in its underlying assumption that human well-being and progress depended entirely on "outward" legal, political and economic arrangements. In a reasonably advanced society such arrangements are sufficient for the protection of material interests; but they are not instruments of social education, they do not really develop men's habits and characters, they thus make no contribution to inherent human improvement. It was, Mill believed, one of the principal merits of the Germano-Coleridgian school of thinkers "to see in the character of the national education existing in any

---

[27] "Bentham" *op,cit.,* p.102.
[28] "Remarks on Bentham's Philosophy", *op.cit.,* p.60.
[29] *Ibid.,* p.51.

political society, at once the principal cause of its permanence as a society, and the chief source of its progressiveness: the former by the extent to which that education operated as a system of restraining discipline; the latter by the degree in which it called forth and invigorated the active faculties."[30] According to Mill, a science or philosophy of national character must form the basis of a social philosophy. He had, at one time, great hopes for this new science, which he dubbed "ethology," or the science of the "laws of the formation of national character."[31] Ethology, he describes as the science which corresponds to the art of education. Education is to be understood in the very wide sense as including the training given by the entire system of social arrangements which form individual and national character. By means of the science of ethology Mill hoped to obtain those sociological laws which he believed to be indispensable to any social philosophy that could be useful both in preserving a stable society and in guiding mankind in a progressive direction.

---

[30] "Coleridge" in Himmelfarb, *op.cit.,* p.145.
[31] *Logic, op.cit.,* Book VI, Ch.V, Sec.4, p.567.

CHAPTER III

MORALITY AND INDIVIDUAL IDEALS

Morality and the Ideal of Individual Development

My argument has been that in a number of earlier essays Mill had already formulated a conception of the good life he was to develop more fully in later writings. In saying this I do not, however, mean to suggest that Mill everywhere adheres consistently to the double-aspect theory of morality. Some hesitation in his use of the word 'morality' has already been remarked upon. Of much greater moment is the fact that towards the end of his essay on Bentham he tacitly abandons the view that self-culture is the highest or even a co-equal aspect of morality. Here he suggests, in effect, that it is not, properly speaking, part of morality at all. Mill's mature view of the relationship between morality and individual ideals will be considered again when I come to examine his principle of self-protection. A preliminary clarification of this relationship is, however, called for at this stage.

In Mill's account of Bentham's position, morality is, according to Bentham's view of it, essentially concerned with the business side of social arrangements. As we have seen, this is the view which Mill criticises in several of his earlier essays. Yet it is very close to the account of morality he himself came finally to adopt. My argument will be that Mill's mature theory of the good life may best be understood as an attempt (albeit not an entirely conscious attempt) to achieve a synthesis between the older utilitarian, "external" morality of wants or "outward interests" and a morality which takes account of individual ideals of human excellence.[1] In the earlier essays Mill was in general proposing to divide the sphere of *morality* into two complementary parts: one concerned with the regulation of

---
[1] Mill's proposal is thus very close to the double-aspect conception of the good life put forward by P.F. Strawson in "Social Morality and Individual Ideal", *Philosophy,* Vol.XXXVI, No.136, January, 1961. Cf. R.M. Hare, *Freedom and Reason* (Oxford, 1963), p.121, pp.123-24, pp.146-53.

outward interests by means of moral and legal rules, the other with the growth and perfection of individual character. This use of the word "morality" he later definitely abandons in favour of a use that relates to a more limited, 'social' conception of the realm of the moral. The reasons for this revision are not entirely clear. No doubt the revision had a good deal to do with the distinction he came to draw between higher and lower desires, a distincion which was to become the foundation of his ideal of the good life. He may well have felt that the word 'morality' was customarily reserved for the social (outward) concept, so that his dual aspect concept of morality, (involving such strong emphasis on personal development) could only inappropriately and misleadingly be associated with the word 'morality'. He may also have thought his own doctrine would be more easily understood and more readily distinguishable from orthodox Benthamism if it were framed not as a double-aspect theory of morality but as a theory of human life and action such as to mark off severally the boundaries of the moral, aesthetic and prudential. I would speculate that the main reason for the revision was his coming to see the social morality of modern, mass societies as unduly oppressive and constrictive, and thus to believe personal liberty could best be protected by drawing a firm dividing line between self-regarding conduct, designated as non-moral, and other-regarding conduct, designated as moral. However that may be, Mill's later doctrine is conceptually (as distinct from terminologically) similar to his earlier one, though it is true there is some elaboration and enrichment. The basic division between conduct as it affects social regulation (elaborated so as to be understood as involving interests in their relation to rights and duties) and conduct as it affects self-culture (elaborated to embrace the self-development of the individual according to his personal ideal of the good life) is preserved. In the later terminology, however, what is on the social side of the dividing line appropriates the word 'morality' to itself, while what is on the individual side is no longer said to be part of the 'moral' realm but is said to belong to a 'prudential/aesthetic' realm.

The texts in which Mill's three-fold division of human conduct is to be found are "Bentham", the *Logic*, *Auguste Comte and Positivism*, *Utilitarianism* and *On Liberty*. Some of the issues involved are touched on by J.O. Urmson[2] and D.D. Raphael[3]. Their remarks on Mill's view of commendable activities have been followed up more recently by a number of writers who have offered, on the basis of Mill's view of commendable activities, a new interpretation of his famous principle of self-protection.[4] This principle is a classical formulation of "the liberal point of view".[5] Hart and most other liberal writers have understood the liberal view as an attempt to defend an area of "'private morality and immorality which in brief and crude terms is not the law's business.'"[6] And Mill's principle has traditionally been seen as an effort to draw a line between the moral and legal realms so as to establish an absolute barrier to social and legal interference with private moral/immoral conduct; in Mill's terms this last is conduct which does not injure the interests of others. The traditional interpretation of the principle has now been challenged. It has been contended that self-regarding conduct falls within the aesthetic or prudential realm and thus is neither moral nor immoral, but non-moral. Other-regarding conduct, however, falls within the moral/legal sphere and so may be subject to sanctions. Hence Mill's principle "is not a distinction between law and morality, but between the sort of conduct subject to law-or-morality on the one hand and that which is subject to neither of these but to prudential or aesthetic appraisal on the other."[7] I shall follow this general line of interpretation in the remainder of this Chapter and also in Chapters X and XI when I come to examine more fully Mill's views on the scope and limits of liberty. In that later context, I shall, however, diverge somewhat from more particular constructions placed on certain parts of Mill's theory by a number of these recent writers.

---

[2] J.O. Urmson, "The Moral Philosophy of J.S. Mill," in Philippa Foot (ed.) *Theories of Ethics* (Oxford, 1967) p.135.
[3] D.D. Raphael "Fallacies in and About Mill's Utilitarianism," *Philosophy* (1955) pp.345-46.
[4] Marcus Singer, *Generalisation in Ethics* (New York, 1961), especially pp.311-18; Alan Ryan, *op. cit.,* and also his "John Stuart Mill's Art of Living," *The Listener,* October 21st, 1965, pp.620-22; A.R. Louch, "Sins and Crimes", *Philosophy,* Vol.XLIII, January, 1968.
[5] H.L.A. Hart, "Immorality and Treason," *The Listener,* Vol.62, No.1583, pp.162-63.
[6] *Ibid.,* p.162. Hart is here quoting from the Wolfenden Committee Report on Homosexual Offences.
[7] A. Ryan, "John Stuart Mill's Art of Living," *op.cit.,* p.620.

Mill's Three-fold Division of Human Conduct

A shift of Mill's opinion concerning what is properly to be called 'morality' can be seen near the end of his essay on Bentham. Here he accuses Bentham of treating the moral aspect of action and character as if it were the only one and overlooking its aesthetic and sympathetic aspects. "Every human action," Mill now maintains, "has three aspects: its *moral* aspect, or that of its *right* and *wrong;* its *aesthetic* aspect, or that of its beauty; its *sympathetic* aspect, or that of its loveableness... According to the first, we approve or disapprove; according to the second, we admire or despise; according to the third, we love, pity, or dislike. The morality of an action depends upon its foreseeable consequences; its beauty, and its loveableness, or the reverse, depend upon the qualities which it is evidence of."[8] Mill seems here to have surrendered his earlier view according to which "an essential part of the morality or immorality of an action or a rule of action consists in its influence upon the agent's own mind." For by "foreseeable consequences" he evidently means what in his "Remarks on Bentham's Philosophy" he called "specific consequences," i.e. the "consequences to which that very action, if practised generally, would itself lead." Thus, from the moral viewpoint, lies would be counted wrong because they mislead and tend to destroy men's confidence in one another; and they would be judged aesthetically objectionable because they are mean and arise out of a cowardly or devious character. (Loveableness, a category mentioned by Mill only to be quickly dropped, seems to relate just to affectionate characteristics). In short, Mill's former criticism of Bentham for failing to include among the moral consequences of actions their effects on the agent's own character is now translated into the objection that he overlooked their aesthetic aspect. (It should be remembered that for Mill 'aesthetic' connotes not only beautiful, but also noble, a connotation which has tended to drop out of modern parlance.)

R.J. Halliday[9] has correctly pointed out that in the course of his discussion of "Bentham" Alan Ryan wrongly attributes Bentham's view of morality to Mill. Ryan states that for Mill morality is "essentially concerned with the business side of life, with preserving minimal forebearances."

---

[8] "Bentham", *op.cit.,* p.116. Italics in original.
[9] R.J. Halliday, *op.cit.,* p.9.

Halliday argues that having misunderstood the essay Ryan cannot use it to support his interpretation of Mill, according to which for Mill morality is concerned with minimal forebearances so that where the agent only is involved the matter is not a moral one. But, in arguing thus, Halliday reveals that he has himself failed to appreciate the full complexity of Mill's doctrine as it appears in "Bentham". Halliday sees that in "Bentham" Mill conceived of "self-education as the first part of morality."[10] But to leave the matter there is to oversimplify. As I have pointed out, towards the end of his essay Mill places self-education in the realm of the aesthetic or noble. This later view is, furthermore, the view that has his allegiance in subsequent writings.

Now Ryan does err in making the slip Halliday points to, but in view of the circumstances I have set out it can be seen that Ryan could have made his case good without in any way leaning on his error. His case can be repaired, since there is in fact some support for his interpretation in "Bentham".

Mill's view of the three aspects of assessment of human activity first introduced in "Bentham" reappears in an altered guise in the *Logic* where he is discussing the Art of Life. He retains the moral and aesthetic aspects of human activity, but the sympathetic disappears and is replaced by the expedient or prudent. The principles of practical (as contrasted with scientific) activity can, he says, be thought of as forming "a body of doctrine, which is properly the Art of Life, in its three departments, Morality, Prudence or Policy, and Aesthetics; the Right, the Expedient, and the Beautiful or Noble, in human conduct and works."[11] He goes on to say that though in the main, an art of life remains to be created, it is possible to indicate the relationship of its three branches to the happiness of man, which is "the ultimate principle of Teleology." According to Mill, the ultimate aim in all three departments of the art of life is the happiness of mankind. Human happiness, in short, is the very general princple to which all principles of practice in the three departments of the right, the prudent, and the beautiful or noble must ultimately conform. And in a footnote[12] Mill adds that the purpose of *Utilitarianism* is to vindicate the view that the happiness of

---

[10] *Ibid.,* p.10.
[11] *Logic, op.cit.,* Book VI, Chapter XII, Sec.7, p.620.
[12] *Ibid.,* p.621 fn.

human life is the ultimate justification for the arts of morality, prudence and aesthetics.

In *Auguste Comte and Positivism* Mill offers some further remarks bearing on the relationship between the province of morality and the area of non-moral evaluation. He complains of the mistake of the Calvinist theory in supposing "that whatever is not a duty is a sin. It does not perceive that between the region of duty and that of sin there is an intermediate space, the region of positive worthiness... There is a standard of altruism to which all should be required to come up and a degree beyond it which is not obligatory but meritorious. It is incumbent on every one to restrain the pursuit of his personal objects within the limits consistent with the essential interests of others. What those limits are, it is the province of ethical science to determine; and to keep all individuals and aggregations of individuals within them, is the proper office of punishment and moral blame."[13]

Then, in *Utilitarianism,* where he is giving an account of the concept of moral obligation, Mill again fixes his attention on the distinction between the realm of morality and that of worthiness:

> "We do not call anything wrong, unless we mean to imply that a person ought to be punished in some way or another for doing it; if not by law, by the opinion of his fellow creatures; if not by opinion, by the reproaches of his own conscience. This seems to me the real turning point of the distinction between morality and simple expediency. It is a part of the notion of Duty in every one of its forms, that a person may be rightfully compelled to fulfil it. Duty is a thing which may be *exacted* from a person, as one exacts a debt. Unless we think that it may be exacted from him, we do not call it his duty. Reasons of prudence, or the interest of other people, may militate against actually exacting it; but the person himself, it is clearly understood, would not be entitled to complain. There are other things on the contrary, which we wish that people should do, which we like or admire them for doing, perhaps dislike or depise them for not doing, but yet admit that they are not bound to do; it is not a case of moral obligation; we do not blame them, that is, we do not think that they are proper objects of punishment. . . we call any conduct wrong. . . according as we think that the person ought, or ought not, to be punished for it; and we say it would be right to do so and so, or merely that it would be desirable or laudable, according as we would wish to see

---

[13] *Auguste Comte and Positivism,* (Michigan, 1961) pp.142-43.

the person whom it concerns, compelled, or only persuaded and exhorted, to act in that manner."[14]

Finally, in the *Liberty*, by distinguishing between self-regarding and other-regarding actions, Mill seeks to elaborate and defend the distinction between the conception of morality and that of commendable activity. He argues that in activities concerning only the individual himself morality is not involved: actions which do not endanger or harm the interests of others are not properly subject either to legal or to moral sanctions. He contends "First, that the individual is not accountable to society for his actions, in so far as these concern the interests of no person but himself. . . Secondly, that for such actions as are prejudicial to the interests of others, the individual is accountable, and may be subjected either to social or to legal punishment, if society is of the opinion that either the one or the other is requisite for its protection."[15] Actions within the self-regarding realm "may be proofs of any amount of folly, or want of personal dignity and self-respect; but they are only a subject of moral reprobation when they involve a breach of duty to others."[16] Mill goes on to argue that the performance of "what are called duties to ourselves" is either a matter of prudence or of "self-respect or self-development".[17] Unless foolish or ignoble behaviour involves "offence against the rights of others" (and so becomes of moral concern), the individual cannot legitimately be held accountable to society for such conduct.

Enough has now been done to sketch Mill's account of his division of human conduct as between the realms of the moral, the prudential, and the aesthetic or noble. This general doctrine will be further discussed in Chapters X and XI where I discuss Mill's principle of self-protection. I now direct attention to the third of Mill's realms of human conduct. In this realm are found ideals of human excellence and in particular Mill's own ideal of "self-development".

---

[14] U, p.45; italics in original.
[15] OL, pp.149-59.
[16] *Ibid.*, p.135.
[17] *Ibid.*

CHAPTER IV

SELF-DEVELOPMENT AND INDIVIDUALITY

Happiness and Self-Development

Mill's individualism - the movement of his thought away from orthodox Benthamism towards an Aristotelian-type ethics of self-development - rises directly to the surface of his writings in the second chapter of *Utilitarianism.* There he attempts to broaden his utilitarianism further by distinguishing between higher and lower pleasures. Of Mill's three significant amendments to Benthamite utilitarianism, this is the most radical and has the most far-reaching implications for Mill's liberalism.

Mill introduces his famous distinction in attempting to meet the charge that utilitarianism is a philosophy fit only for pigs. Bentham certainly admitted (same-level) qualitative differences between pleasures and indeed provided a classification of the different sorts of pleasure. On the other hand, Bentham could not concede any such distinction as that between *higher* and *lower* pleasures for to have done so would have rendered his hedonistic calculus completely unworkable. To Bentham, "quantity of pleasures being equal, pushpin is as good as poetry". Yet according to Mill one can speak of certain pleasures as "higher" or superior to others even though they afford less pleasure i.e. in Bentham's terms are less intense, less permanent and so forth.

Mill's crucial claims are: (1) A distinction must be drawn between the "two very different ideas, of happiness and content" (where *content,* or *contentment* means *satisfaction*); and (2) Happiness essentially involves "a sense of dignity" and the exercise and cultivation of the higher faculties. Thus Mill is claiming that in order for men and women to be happy it is necessary for them to enjoy "the pleasures of the intellect, of the feelings and imagination, and of the moral sentiments." "Human beings", he maintains, "have faculties more elevated than the animal appetites, and when once made conscious of them do not regard anything as happiness which does not include their gratification". An inferior person whose pleasures are confined to those of the bodily appetites may be more contented or satisfied than a more cultivated person is, but he will not be happier. Conversely, someone who is capable of enjoying the higher pleasures of life may not necessarily be as contented as the more ordinary person, but his life will be a happier one.[1]

In these passages a strong Aristotelian strain comes to the surface of Mill's thought, a strain quite at variance with the hedonistic utilitarianism of Bentham. Mill is here saying it *is better* to live on a higher than a lower plane; he is placing a high value on the pleasures of the intellect, the imagination and the feelings and a comparatively low value on the pleasures of the senses. It is better to live on a higher plane because intellectual activity, the exercise of moral responsibility and the cultivation of the sensibilities always produce more happiness - though in terms of contentment or satisfaction, they may sometimes even be painful: "It is better to be a human being dissatisfied than a pig satisfied: better to be Socrates dissatisfied than a fool satisfied."[2]

It must, however, be conceded that Mill's argument in *Utilitarianism* unwinds unsystematically and with what is at times an infuriating inconsistency. In discriminating between mental and bodily pleasures, though, it is evident he is allowing into his theory a distinction involving a clear departure from a strict hedonistic utilitarianism. Bentham and James Mill were, in general, willing to equate happiness with pleasure, and pleasure with the satisfaction of a chain of desires. For Bentham, in assessing happiness our only criterion ought to be the gratification of as many desires as possible, since the only consideration was to be the gratification of wants or desires as such and all desires were considered to be on a level. That action would be counted best, then, which on balance leads to the most pleasure, that is to say the most intense and lasting satisfaction or enjoyment. By contrast, Mill says that though lower pleasures may afford us greater satisfaction or contentment, we cannot really be happy (as distinct from satisfied) unless we experience the superior pleasures of life. But once this is admitted Mill's contention that a qualitative ranking of pleasures is "quite compatible with the principle of

---

[1] The pasages quoted above are from U, pp.7-9.
[2] U, p.9.

utility",³ can be seen to be unacceptable. If "utility" is understood in Bentham's sense, namely as the principle according to which pleasure or satisfaction is the only thing desirable as an end, then the distinction between qualitatively higher and lower pleasures amounts to an abandonment of that principle. In admitting that the higher pleasures are intrinsically superior even though bringing less contentment, Mill is letting into his theory an additional criterion of goodness by which contentment or satisfaction may *itself* be evaluated.

The truth is that Mill's use of the term "happiness" in *Utilitarianism* is ambiguous. On occasions his usage is strictly hedonistic: By "happiness" is meant "pleasure and the absence of pain";⁴ a man by this reckoning is counted happy if he experiences as many as possible of the pleasures he would like to experience, no matter what their character and thus he is happy if he gratifies the desires *he* deems important. But when Mill insists we cannot be happy unless we experience the particular pleasures associated with *the exercise of our higher faculties,* he tacitly abandons the hedonistic notion of happiness and replaces it with a eudaemonist conception. By "happiness" he now means simply the experience of those superior pleasures supervening upon the exercise of our higher faculties. And he proceeds to contrast this conception with the very different conception of "satisfaction" or contentment, which is the feeling we experience when we are enjoying the lower or inferior pleasures.

Mill's concept of happiness as the ultimate good for man, resembles, I am saying, Aristotle's *eudaemonia,* set forth in Book I of the *Nichomachean Ethics.* Both conceive happiness as compatible with some degree of dissatisfaction. Both insist happiness is not to be equated with pleasure if by that is meant the satisfaction of a train of bodily appetites - for food, drink, sex, comfort and so forth. Again, happiness on their understanding of the term, is not merely the experience of a series of highly pleasurable but ephemeral feelings. The happiness which Mill has in mind, he says, is "not a life of rapture; but moments of such, in an existence made up of few and transitory pains, many and various pleasures, with a decided predominance of the active over the passive."⁵ Above all, Mill thinks that a

---

³ *Ibid.,* p.7.
⁴ *Ibid.,* p.6.
⁵ U, p.12.

person can attain a happy life only by exercising his peculiarly human capacities, which in being exercised develop and flourish. For a person to lead a happy life he must actively and rationally pursue certain "ideal ends". Mill's argument is that though men share with other animals the desire for sensual indulgence and gratification of the bodily appetites, desire, that is to say, for "mere satisfaction", they differ from animals in possessing what he describes as a "sense of dignity" in some, "though by no means in exact, proportion to their higher faculties". Once men become conscious of their potentiality for developing their higher powers they cannot really be happy unless they are able to lead the sort of life in which those powers are cultivated and perfected. In *Utilitarianism,* then, Mill is not by any means a strict or consistent hedonist. He has moved away from the hedonism of Bentham towards an ethics which has as its starting point the conception of the highly developed individual.

The most highly developed persons will be those who have starved none of their higher capacities, since self-development is a matter of preserving a "due balance among the faculties". Mill deplores any doctrine which emphasizes the development of intellectual power and moral judgment at the expense of the cultivation of human feelings and the sharpening of artistic perceptions.[6] The young Mill himself provides an example of the imbalance the mature Mill deplores. Before his mental crisis at the age of twenty, Mill was a man of impressive intellectual powers. Even so, he had a deep sense of how greatly his personality was enriched when, after discovering the poetry of Wordsworth, he became preoccupied for a time with "the cultivation of the feelings" and came gradually to appreciate the role of personal sensitivity and aesthetic appreciation in the good life.

By contending that the pleasure derived from the nobler capacities is intrinsically superior Mill is, then, tacitly admitting that something other than pleasure is the sole good. Moreover, what he is saying can only be understood by reference to the nature of certain *activities;* it is not possible to characterise the higher pleasures except by referring to the nature of the intellectual, moral, imaginative and emotional capacities from which they are derived. Thus, it is possible to interpret Mill's qualitative distinction between pleasures as a distinction not between pleasures but between

---

[6] *Autobiography, op.cit.,* p.101, c.f. *Auguste Comte and Positivism, op.cit.,* p.117.

activities.[7] Furthermore, as we have seen, the "higher faculties" with which the superior pleasures are correlated, are themselves selected as being higher on the ground that they are peculiar to man. Though Mill may not have been fully aware of what he was about in this section of *Utilitarianism*, it is clear that his qualitative distinction between pleasures turns on the concept of man adumbrated in his earlier critique of Bentham's inadequate concept of human nature. Mill, it is true, never formally abandoned the view that pleasure and the absence of pain is the sole criterion of morality. But it can be seen that he nevertheless invokes an antecedent conception of man and of his characteristic excellence, a conception which is the real foundation of his theory of the good life. This ulterior foundation can be descried even more clearly in *On Liberty*, to which I now turn.

Self-Development and Individuality

In *Utilitarianism* Mill's purpose was to justify and defend utilitarianism, and his picture of human nature is drawn mainly in hedonistic terms. As we should expect, the position is rather different when we turn to the *Liberty*. It is significant that his fullest and most explicit account of self-development as the ultimate end of human life should occur in *On Liberty* where he is expressly concerned to enunciate and defend a theory of freedom. An element of hedonistic utilitarianism is still discernible, but accompanying it is a fuller and sharper enunciation of the conception of human nature and morality which is at the foundation of his liberalism. The central notion of Mill's ethic ceases to be pleasure and becomes that of a good man.

Mill informs us in the Introduction to his essay that even though he proposes to take his stand on the principle of utility "It must be utility in the largest sense, grounded on the permanent interests of man as a progressive being."[8] Regrettably, he does not then go on to provide his

---

[7] On this point see R.S. Downie, "Mill on Pleasure and Self-Development", *Philosophical Quarterly*, Vol.16, No.62, pp.69-71.

[8] *On Liberty* (Everyman edition, 1910) p.74. All succeeding references to *On Liberty* will be to this edition, which will be represented by the abbreviation OL.

readers with a complete or systematic account of those "permanent interests". Still, we have already been able to build up a preliminary sketch of them, drawing on the *Autobiography,* "Remarks on Bentham's Philosophy", "Bentham" and *Utilitarianism;* the details of that picture emerge much more clearly once we turn to the *Liberty* and especially to Chapter III on individuality.

Mill tells us in his *Autobiography* that his essay *On Liberty* is "a kind of philosophic text-book of a single truth. . . the importance to man and society, of a large variety in types of character, and of giving full freedom to human nature to expand itself in innumerable and conflicting directions."[9] He takes as the motto for his essay this quotation from Wilhelm von Humboldt's *Sphere and Duties of Government:*

> "The grand leading principle towards which every argument unfolded on these pages directly converges, is the absolute and essential importance of human development in its richest diversity."[10]

In the essay itself, he appeals specifically to von Humboldt's doctrine and to the "Greek ideal of self-development;" and in summarising his vindication of self-development asks: "what more or better can be said of any condition of human affairs than that it brings human beings themselves nearer to the best thing they can be."[11] In stressing the importance of persons developing in their own distinctive ways he takes himself to be championing "the doctrine of the rights of individuality, and the claim of the moral nature to develop itself in its own way."[12] Individuality should be promoted, he explains, because it is "one of the principal ingredients of human happiness, and quite the chief ingredient of individual and social progress;" and as well as being one of the "leading essentials of well-being," it is also "a necessary part and condition" of "civilization, instruction, education, culture."[13] Taken together these passages provide us with a number of clues to what Mill understands by individuality and as to what he sees as the key inter-relationships between happiness, self-development, and individuality.

---

[9] *Autobiography, op.cit.,* p.177.
[10] OL, p.62.
[11] OL pp.120, 121.
[12] *Autobiography, op.cit.,* p.179.
[13] OL p.115.

With the idea of individuality we reach the heart of Mill's liberalism. His liberalism rests on a belief in self-development, or self-perfection, as the highest object man can pursue, and self-development is intimately linked with individuality in that individuality is taken to be both the principal condition of and the chief ingredient in the developed or perfected self. But what is 'individuality'? The terms 'individual' and 'individuality' are among the commonest terms to be found in the writings of English liberal thinkers. Yet we seldom find any attempt to analyse their meaning or even much awareness that this is essential for an understanding of the liberal position. Unfortunately, Mill, too, talks about the notion in a somewhat discursive way and makes no effort to provide a systematic account of it. Even so, his chapter "On Individuality" in the *Liberty,* along with the other remarks he makes in the same essay and elsewhere, provide the materials for an explication of the concept. With the exercise of a little perseverance we can identify the type of human conduct and the sorts of relationships Mill evidently has in mind when he talks about individuality. For, apart from a troublesome ambiguity to be discussed later, he does succeed well enough in indicating what he means by 'individuality', how it is connected with self-development and why it should be regarded as the most essential of man's interests.

Criteria for Individuality

In what, we may ask, does individuality consist? What is it about an individual that enables us to regard him as a being distinguishable from his fellows and capable of leading a life of his own? What criterion or criteria do we implicitly rely upon when as a matter of ordinary behaviour we distinguish one person from another?

One obvious criterion is that of discreteness; we ordinarily have no difficulty in distinguishing one human being as a distinct physical object. Another criterion would be that of distinctive physical charcteristics: people differ one from another in size, shape, facial appearance, physical strength, and in other measurable physical respects. Yet even though human beings can be distinguished from one another by their discreteness and particular constellation of physical features, we should not normally wish to say that therefore they possess individuality. Since all people are in a generic sense individuals (can be identified as separate beings contained within different skins and having a special set of physical characteristics) their being individuals in this generic sense is completely unremarkable. Moreover, all people *simply* have individuality in this sense. it is not a sense that admits of degree.

What of the sense in which one finds it necessary to say that some people are individuals whilst others are not, or that some have *more* individuality than others? For Mill, individuality is something which may be developed, so he certainly assumes that some sense can be attached to the notion of one person being more of an individual than another. "Persons of genius," he avers, are "more individual than any other people".[14] Yet this makes no sense if we are talking about individuality only in the numerical sense of the term. Again, Mill notes that the people of a particular nation may cease to possess individuality and bemoans the fact that in the England of his day society may be said to have "fairly got the better of individuality".[15] He is clearly not speaking of mere numerical difference when he expresses acute anxiety about the decline of individuality.

Evidently one meaning of 'individuality' may be invoked in determining that a human being is an individual in a numerical sense and a further meaning may, as it were, be superimposed upon the first when it is intended to refer to degrees of individuality. This assumption of Mill's is also made by a number of others who have written on the subject of individualism and individuality; e.g. it underlies the contention that human individuality was either non-existent or exceedingly weak in early historical cultures and emerged later at a specific place and period.[16] Thus Michael Oakeshott has asserted that "human individuality is an historical emergence", which, though it might on occasions have been enjoyed intermittently in the distant past, first became firmly established in Western Europe towards the close of the thirteenth century.[17] Again, some writers

---

[14] *Ibid.,* p.122.
[15] *Ibid.,* p.119.
[16] See especially Jacob Burkard, *The Civilization of the Renaissance in Italy* (London, 1921); W. Hocking, *The Lasting Elements of Individualism* (Yale University Press, 1937); Erich Fromm, *Fear of Freedom* (London, 1960); M. Oakeshott, *op.cit.*
[17] Oakeshott, *op.cit.,* p.152.

claim to detect a similar emergence of individuality in the life history of the individual, for whereas the new-born baby is an organically separate creature, it is only when he is older that we begin to ascribe to him any genuine individuality. Furthermore, when we use the term 'individuality' in ordinary speech we appear to do so in this comparative sense. When comparing two men we may, for instance, say of one that he 'has individuality' and of another that he has not. What seems to be involved here is the possession by one man of characteristics virtually lacking in the other. The term 'individuality' is, then, a comparative one and susceptible of degree, so that if persons were ranked along a continuum, those at one end would exhibit a very low degree of individuality whereas those at the other end would display a high degree of individuality. Perhaps this does not yet take us very far, though it does at least seem quite consistent with what we assume or have in mind when in ordinay speech we say of someone that he is an individual or has individuality.

    The problem which now arises is that of specifying the criterion or criteria for ranking persons on the individuality scale. When we compare one man with another and conclude that the first has individuality while the second has not, it is clear that we must be comparing them in respect of certain characteristics and not others. What *are* these characteristics? On what grounds do we select some features rather than others as the basis of comparison? In the first place, it would seem that the characteristics we choose will depend upon what we regard as an important difference between human beings. And what we regard as an important difference will, in turn, depend upon our overall scheme of values, our practical, intellectual and moral beliefs. In Mill's case we shall find that his concept of individuality is connected with what has previously been characterised as his moral individualism.[18] The particular meaning he gives to the concept of the individual derives from the fundamental assumption embodied in the doctrine of moral individualism. The assumption is that a man is not to be regarded as an individual unless he is an independent moral agent, with the power of making his own judgments and acting according to his own conscience. This point will emerge more clearly if we continue to follow up certain clues in Mill's discussion of individuality.

---

[18] *Supra,* pp.13-16.

Individuality, Self-Determination and Relative Difference

In Mill's essay *On Liberty* the term 'individuality' is commonly associated with the notions of independence and unlikeness. Thus he links individuality with "individual independence", "individual spontaneity", "spontaneity", the "power" or "sovereignty" of the individual over himself; and he also connects it with "variety", "unlikeness", lack of "uniformity" in thought and character. Men and women with individuality are those who put into the conduct of their lives an impress of "their own judgment" and of "their own individual character".[19] Such men and women possess "sovereignty" over themselves; what they think or do is not merely the outcome of social controls, of "social" or "customary" morality backed by the forces of education, public opinion and the state. They are, in short, autonomous, or self-determining. Such persons think, feel and act *independently;* their opinions, desires, impluses and conduct can, therefore, readily be *distinguished* from that of their fellows. When a man is displaying individuality, his beliefs and actions will not conform to what is considered to be the normal standard; they will be recognised as being in some notable respects *unlike* those of ordinary men and women. Thus independence and unlikeness are bound up together; where there is independence of thought and conduct there will normally be considerable variations in the thought and behaviour of individuals. So understood, the prime value of individuality is fundamental to Mill's moral outlook. The requirement that individuals should be treated as capable of making their own judgments and decisions and left free to make up their own minds concerning what they are to believe or to do is the cornerstone of Mill's moral individualism.

In invoking the criteria of the relative independence and relative uniqueness of the self, Mill isolates two principal elements of the ordinary use of 'individuality'. These criteria are also the two most frequently invoked by a number of more recent liberal theorists.[20] Moreover, understood in this sense the concept of individuality may be *identified* with

---

[19] OL, p.116.
[20] One has in mind here such thinkers as A.D. Lindsay, Ernest Barker, R.M. Maciver, John Dewey, R.B. Perry, and Erich Fromm.

that of freedom in the sense of self-determination. The type of freedom to which Mill is most deeply committed is self-determination, or individuality, since this is for him both the main condition of and the chief ingredient in the perfected or developed self. Freedom in this sense is not a relational concept; it does not stand for a relation between persons, but for a dispositional property of persons. This is Berlin's positive sense of freedom, which "derives from the wish on the part of the individual to be his own master". I am free, in this sense, if "my life and decisions depend on myself, not on external forces of whatever kind," if I am "the instrument of my own, not of other men's acts of will". I am free if "I wish to be a subject, not an object; to be moved by reasons, by conscious purposes, which are my own, not by causes which affect me, as it were, from outside. I wish to be. . . a doer - deciding, not being decided for, self-directed and not acted upon by external nature or by other men as if I were a thing, or an animal, or a slave incapable of playing a human role, that is, of conceiving goods and policies of my own and realising them."[21] In Mill's view, individuality stands for the capacity of the individual to determine his own line of conduct, to direct his life without being impeded or interfered with by other individuals and without being inhibited by the controls of law, custom, convention and public opinion. Yet it is still often said of Mill that he thought of freedom in a purely 'negative' way; that he identified freedom simply with the absence of compulsion by state or society. This assumption may well have arisen from Mill's practice of using the word "individuality" to mean freedom in the sense of self-determination.

It is true that Mill frequently equates freedom with non-interference. It is also true that he always regards negative freedom as part of liberty. At the same time, Mill, in effect, extended the concept of liberty by adding to the traditional, negative concept of freedom the idea of individuality, newly elaborated by himself. He does so in the course of facing up to the problem of conformism within the context of a newly emerging mass society. In order to explore more fully Mill's conception of individuality it thus becomes necessary to turn now to his discussion of freedom and conformity in the mass society.

---

[21] Sir Isiah Berlin, *Two Concepts of Liberty* (Oxford 1958) p.16.

CHAPTER V

INDIVIDUALITY, FREEDOM AND THE TYRANNY OF THE MAJORITY

Negative and Positive Freedom

Negative freedom is, I repeat, part of Millian liberty. When Mill uses the word "freedom" or the word "liberty" in *On Liberty* it does frequently carry the commonsense meaning which we derive from the British empiricist tradition and associate with Hobbes, Locke and Bentham. In this use, often regarded as the primary sense of 'liberty', a man's impulses or desires are taken as the given data and what is in question is whether any constraints stop him giving effect to them. ". . . liberty", Mill claims, "consists in doing what one desires. . ."[1] It is clear that in this context, and in a good many others as well, he thinks of liberty as jeopardised only by external or direct forms of constraint. He is concerned in the essay, he explains, with "the dealings of society with the individual in the way of compulsion and control, whether the means used be physical force in the form of legal penalties or the moral coercion of public opinion."[2] Thus a person is unfree, is not doing what he desires, when sanctions are being invoked against him, whether these take the form of laws backed by the force of the state or assume the form of outright moral prohibitions supported by the sanctions of social opinion - "the tyranny of the prevailing opinion and feeling".[3]

But Mill could not rest content with altogether relying upon the negative concept of freedom. The originality of his *Essay* lies very much in the fact that, without making it quite explicit what he is doing, he extended the older liberal concept of freedom. He wrote the *Essay* at a time when certain characteristics emerging in nineteenth century society seemed to him to thrust the problem of liberty into a wholly new perspective. Earlier liberal theory, he believed, had become partly outmoded because of its

---

[1] OL, p.152.
[2] *Ibid.*, p.72; see also pp.73-74, p.150.
[3] *Ibid.*, p.68.

failure to take these changes into account. Mill, in much of his social and political writing and especially in the *Liberty,* was preoccupied with what appeared to him to be the inexorable advance of social conformity in modern European communities. From his study of De Tocqueville's *Democracy in America* and from his own observations and reflections, he concluded that modern, industrial democracies were rapidly becoming more egalitarian and generating pressures hostile to the growth and extension of individuality. He became fearful "lest the inevitable growth of social equality and of the government of public opinion, should impose on mankind an oppressive yoke of uniformity in opinion and practice."[4]

His discernment of a powerful historical trend towards the growth of a mass society with its extreme egalitarianism and stress on social conformity leads Mill to attempt a restatement of the problem of liberty. The "changes progressively taking place in modern society" have led to a situation where "in the stage of progress into which the more civilized portions of the species have now entered, it [the question of "social liberty"] presents itself under new conditions, and requires a different and more fundamental treatment."[5] He then goes on (in the Introduction to his *Liberty*) to explain what these new conditions are and why they call for a new approach to the problem of liberty. After sketching the long history of the "struggle between Liberty and Authority", he points out that "the tyranny of the majority" operating through the acts of democratic governments has come to be generally recognised both in theory and in practice as constituting the most dangerous threat to liberty. But what only a few reflective persons perceive is that the tyranny of the majority is not confined to the acts of governments and that in England especially, a much more serious danger is to be apprehended from the likings and dislikings of society or the "yoke of opinion." In an eloquent summary of his chief concern in the *Liberty,* Mill writes:

> "Society can and does execute its own mandates: and if it issues wrong mandates instead of right, or any mandates at all in things with which it ought not to meddle, it practices a social tyranny more formidable than many kinds of political oppression, since, though not usually upheld by such extreme penalties, it leaves fewer means of escape, penetrating much more deeply into the details of life, and enslaving the soul itself. Protection, therefore, against the

---

[4] *Autobiography,* op.cit., pp.177-8.
[5] *Ibid.,* p.177; OL, p.65.

tyranny of the magistrate is not enough: there needs protection also against the tyranny of the prevailing opinion and feeling: against the tendency of society to impose by other means than civil penalties, its own ideas and practices as rules of conduct on those who dissent from them: to fetter the development, and if possible prevent the formation, of any individuality not in harmony with its ways, and compel all characters to fashion themselves upon the model of its own. There is a limit to the legitimate interference of collective opinion with individual independence: and to find that limit, and maintain it against encroachment, is as indispensable to a good condition of human affairs, as protection against political despotism."[6]

Mill's enunciation, in the Introduction and in his *Autobiography* of his chief concern in writing the *Liberty*, is confirmed in the body of the essay itself where we find him devoting an entire chapter (Chapter III) to the question of individuality and social interference and a good deal of the following chapter to the same question.

The question now facing Mill was whether the traditional, 'negative' concept of freedom remained adequate for dealing with the problem of freedom within the context of the new mass society. To some extent it could be adapted to deal with the new situation, and part of Mill's treatment of the problem of the tyranny of social opinion reveals just such an adaptation. In his response to the problem of the tyranny of the majority Mill was in part concerned simply with the direct coercion of the individual by society i.e. with moral rules backed by social "penalties" or sanctions. Some but not all of the social tyranny the *Liberty* was especially designed to combat arose from the oppressive social ethos of the Victorian middle class, whose Philistinism and intolerance were reinforced by the theories and projects of many social and religious reformers.

This appeal to the feelings of the majority on moral matters brought into play a "yoke of opinion" which had extremely mischievous effects in at least two notable directions. First, in the area of thought and discussion it induced in many of the most active and inquiring minds an extreme moral timidity. They had a strong inclination to keep their heretical thoughts to themselves and to conceal their true opinions when offering their views to the public. "Our merely social intolerance", says Mill, "kills no one, roots out no opinions, but induces men to disguise them, or to abstain from any

---

[6] OL, p.68.

active effort for their diffusion."[7] Secondly, the tyranny of social opinion is invariably associated with a whole series of active attempts by the majority (or by those who represent themselves as speaking on behalf of the majority) to extend the ambit of "moral police". Strenuous efforts are made to enforce the majority moral viewpoint on those who do not share it, by means of legislation designed to protect people for their own good. Examples discussed by Mill include prohibition, Sabbatarian legislation, and other efforts to restrict public enjoyment and amusements.[8]

A good deal of Mil's discussion of the problem of the social tyranny of the majority is, then, concerned with the need to expose and thereby possibly avert the external, more direct or *perceived* constraints upon individual discussion and personal behaviour which flowed from the oppressive social ethos of Victorian England. But there is something else as well. Richard B. Friedman has recently pointed out that Mill's use in the *Liberty* of expressions like 'social tyranny' and 'social oppression' is ambiguous.[9] They may refer either to external social coercion or to the indirect, unperceived and internalised influences of the prevailing social morality.

I propose now to elaborate on the contrast, to be found in Mill but not brought out in a very explicit way, between, on the one hand, overt social coercion and, on the other hand, social controls of a more indirect kind. There are a number of contexts in which it seems clear Mill is concerned simply with social coercion: for instance, when he says "society can and does execute its own mandates", "society has expended fully as much effort in the attempt (according to its lights) to compel people to conform to its notions of personal as of social excellence"; or when he speaks of "the

---

[7] *Ibid.*, p.93.
[8] *Ibid.*, pp.143-47.
[9] Richard B. Friedman, "A New Exploration of Mill's Essay 'On Liberty' ", *Political Studies,* Vol.14, No.3, October 1966. For part of what follows concerning Mill's departure from the traditional empiricist view of liberty I am indebted to Friedman's careful analysis. Yet in claiming Mill "made no discernible effort to articulate and develop that concept of freedom [i.e. as "self-determination"] in *Liberty"* (p.291) Friedman, though correct up to a point, fails to appreciate that, since 'individuality' and 'self-determination' are equivalent, Mill's chapter on individuality may be read as in part an attempt to articulate the notion of self-determination.

coercion of public opinion".[10] These pronouncements recognise social tyranny as a threat to liberty, but they conceive of social constraint on the analogy of physical and legal constraint. Mill is here still operating with the concept of negative freedom, while extending it to include the interference of public opinion as an additional and (hitherto) underestimated form of external coercion. Liberty is still essentially the absence of external obstacles to the expression of one's desires. The point Mill is laying stress on, though, is that a person's desires may be frustrated as much by the fear of social as of legal threats and deterrents.

But even if a man is free in the negative sense (i.e. is not deterred by threats or sanctions, whatever their source, from doing what he desires) may it not be that, in another sense of 'freedom' he nevertheless remains unfree? For there is a sense of 'freedom' where attention is focussed not on the contraints which a man perceives as obstacles to the realisation of his desires, but on the man himself and on the origin of his opinions and desires. It is this sense of freedom - freedom as self-determination - which Mill has in mind when he introduces the idea of "individuality" in Chapter III of *On Liberty*. His discussion there indicates that, without quite being able to make the point explicit, he has become aware that one of his concepts of liberty - the absence of constraints on doing what one desires - gives a partial, but not a full characterisation of liberty.

A man may be unimpeded by social (or legal) constraints and yet, as Mill came to see, be dominated by a more subtle and much more effective form of social 'tyranny': custom, convention and mass opinion may be operating on him in such a way that he never stops to think where or how he acquired his beliefs or desires and it rarely occurs to him to question them. The majority of men and women ("from the highest class of society down to the lowest") are largely passive in relation to their society; even if they are not coerced by legal or social sanctions, their opinions, tastes and ways of living are largely determined by the prevailing customs, pattern of beliefs and morality of that society. Most people are largely lacking in individuality. They do not ask about a proposed action - "what do I prefer? or, what would suit my character and disposition? or, what would allow the best and highest in me to have fair play, and enable it to grow and thrive?"

---

[10] OL, pp.68, 76, 72. Quoted by Friedman, *op.cit.,* p.288.

They ask: is it suitable to someone in my position or (worse still) in a position superior to my own? "I do not mean," Mill explains, "that they choose what is customary in preference to what suits their own inclination. It does not occur to them to have any inclination, except for what is customary". "Conformity" is the first and only thought of the majority, until through "not following their own nature they have no nature to follow" and "are generally without either opinions or feelings of home growth, or properly their own".[11]

By contrast with the conformist or "mass" man, the person with individuality, the self-determining man, is he whose opinions and desires represent his own personal bent or the path of life he has chosen for himself. As well as being unobstructed by external constraints, his desires are truly *his own;* his opinions, impulses and decisions depend on or flow from his own character;[12] he is more than just a reflector of the dominant customs or conventions of his society. The independent or autonomous person is he who thinks his own thoughts and makes his own decisions over a certain range of his activities. This does not mean he is not in some measure beholden to traditions and customs. People must be trained in youth to benefit by the results of human experience and the mature adult finds some customs both good and suitable to his characater and circumstances. But the free man always has customs and traditions under critical review: he does not "conform to custom, merely *as* custom" for he "who does anything because it is the custom makes no choice."[13] The self-directing man is the person who scrutinises the standards of society, who is fully aware that there are different and competing opinions and ways of life and who strives to judge them critically and to act responsibly on the basis of his judgments.

For Mill, individuality is not mere non-conformity. He is not saying that choice is exercised only in condemning current standards or in

---

[11] The above passages are from OL, p.119.
[12] "A person whose desires and impulses are his own - are the expression of his own nature, as it has been developed and modified by his own culture, is said to have a character. One whose desires and impulses are not his own, has no character, no more than a steam engine has a character." *Ibid.,* p.115. See also pp.115, 119 and cf. *Logic, op.cit.,* p.552.
[13] *Ibid.,* p.116. Italics in original.

continual rebellion against accepted modes of behaviour; it is the act of questioning which, in Mill's view, gives content to the notion of choice. Millian individuality has, however, been taken to mean mere unlikeness or difference. I regard this as a gross misinterpretation and propose to clear Mill of the charge of putting forward the unsophisticated view that would be implied by such a definition. One can see how when Mill stresses the need for non-conformity it might be thought he is assuming individuality to be nothing other than unusual or eccentric thought and behaviour. In these circumstances it is perhaps not too surprising that some of Mill's critics have supposed that uniqueness is, for him, the only criterion of individuality. Thus R.F. Anschutz charges Mill with "the error of assuming that a man is only himself when he succeeds in being different from other men, as if individuality meant peculiarity or idiosyncracy."[14] Such a view, Anschutz suggests, would require Mill to count the mere eccentric - the mindless, weak-willed Bohemian, let us say, - as more of an individual than most people, since he is so obviously more unusual. And Anschutz goes on to argue that we cannot for a moment believe that the man who spends most of his time struggling hard to assimilate the traditions of his calling and conforms, out of conviction, to most of the customs of his community, is any less of an individual than someone whose ruling passion is his desire to revolt against custom and tradition. Now, it is certainly true (as Anschutz is at pains to emphasize) that Mill does speak of the desirability of eccentricity, though with two qualifications Anschutz fails to notice. First, eccentricity, "the mere refusal to bend the knee to custom", should be encouraged only when the tyranny of mass opinion is exceptionally strong - as Mill believed it was in the England of his day; at other times, when the pressure towards social conformity is not so strong, there is no need to encourage exceptional individuals to behave differently from the rest of society. Secondly, in the context about the desirability of eccentricity from which Anschutz quotes, Mill links the desirability of difference with the desirability of *independence* of character. He observes: "Eccentricity has always abounded when and where strength of character has abounded and the amount of eccentricity in a society has generally been proportional to the amount of genius, mental vigour, and moral courage it contained."[15] In other words, Mill is here explicitly connecting uniqueness with mental vigour and strength of character, and linking it to the notion of freedom as

---

[14] R.F. Anschutz, *The Philosophy of J.S. Mill* (Oxford, 1953) p.27.
[15] OL, p.125.

meaning self-determination. He is indicating that where there is mental and moral independence, there will generally be considerable variations in thought and behaviour and that where such variations are absent there is unlikely to be very much independence or autonomy. Mill is in effect postulating a statistically high, but not an invariable, correlation between relative difference and the possession of individuality.

Summing up our discussion of Mill's view of "individuality" we may say, then, that when Mill employs the concept what he usually has in mind is the power or capacity for critical thought and responsible decision. Clearly, he is speaking about and recommending a special type of character or mode of living; what he has in mind is a certain ideal of life to which in any society only a minority of its members closely approximate. On Mill's view, what we mean when we say of someone that he is an individual (or possesses individuality) is that he is a person who has in considerable measure developed his capacity for critical judgment and decision and so can properly be regarded as a distinct human being set apart from his fellow members of society. The mass of men and women are obviously individuals in what we earlier called a generic sense: they can be counted separately and they each possess certain special characteristics which enable us to pick them out from their fellows. But they do not fully qualify as individuals in Mill's sense or (as we might equally well put it) they have a relatively low degree of individuality.

A political philosophy, (it was stated in Chapter I), will on examination be found to contain a more or less explicit picture or conception of man. Mill's doctrine of individuality is part of such a picture; it is his view of what men essentially are or are capable of becoming. What Mill regards as most fundamental in the nature of a man is his capacity for choice and (as a corollary) his relative uniqueness. For Mill the most important though not the only characteristic human excellence is man's individuality, or his capacity for self-determination. As we shall see, the notion of individuality does not exhaust Mill's concept of man; the perfectly developed man has other excellences as well; but individuality is the most essential for it is both the principal condition of and the most vital ingredient in the fully developed personality.

Individuality as
Self-Development?

Consider the following passages, instances of contexts that might give rise to an alternative interpretation of individuality, in which it is equated not with self-determination but with self-development:
"individuality is the same thing with development, and. . . it is only the cultivation of individuality which produces or can produce well-developed human beings.[16]

Or again where Mill approvingly quotes von Humboldt:
"that 'the end of man . . . is the highest and most harmonious development of his powers to a complete and consistent whole;' that, therefore, the object 'towards which very human being must ceaselessly direct his efforts . . . is the individuality of power and development . . .' "[17]

Such passages might seem to suggest that Mill is thinking of self-development and the development of individuality as one and the same thing. P.H. Partridge appears to read Mill in this way in the context where he writes: "For John Mill, the great thing is the full development by each man of his own individuality, his own special capacities of mind, feeling and moral judgment . . ."[18] He suggests that, for Mill, the term "individuality" covers more or less all the distinctive aspects of the self or personality, so that to say of a man that he had developed his individuality would be to say that he had developed or perfected his self.

To grant that his interpretation of Mill's concept of individuality is along the right lines, would not radically alter my own account of Mill's view of the good life. On both renderings, self-determination remains an important element in the good life. The difference resides in the fact that Partridge would interpret Mill's concept of individuality as including such things as the cultivation of the personal and aesthetic feelings: my interpretation of the concept would exclude them from Mill's notion of 'individuality' while allowing that he regards them as an integral part of the developed personality. Since Mill does not fully articulate the concept of individuality it is impossible to be dogmatic concerning the nuances of his view. Nevertheless, the interpretation which would identify individuality

---

[16] *Ibid.,* p.121.
[17] *Ibid.,* pp.115-16.
[18] *On Liberty - A J.S. Mill Centenary* (Current Affairs Bulletin, Department of Tutorial Classes, University of Sydney, 1958) p.8.

with a man's "special capacities of mind, feeling and moral judgment" seems to me to be mistaken for the following reasons.

First, the use of the term 'individuality' which it attributes to Mill is not the one he usually and frequently adopts in the chapter on individuality and in other parts of the *Liberty*. I have shown that in linking individuality with independence and difference what Mill normally has in mind is what we should call self-determination. He is thinking, that is to say, of the acts of judgment and of choice, the excercise of the intellect and the movement of the will through the influences of the "desires and impulses". In Mill's view, a man expresses his individuality when he determines his own course of life, by his own *decisions:* when he is exercising his *critical capacities* in questioning received opinion and when his *actions* are the outcome of reasoned choice.[19]

Secondly, in his *Autobiography* Mill drew a distinction between the "active capacities" and the "passive susceptibilities": by the former he meant both the intellectual abilities (or the analytical and critical powers) and the strength and firmness of the will in moral decision; by the latter he meant the personal sympathies and aesthetic feelings. The active capacities he thought of as being developed by the "training of the human being for speculation and for action" whereas the feelings were nourished and enriched by what he called the "internal culture of the individual", the main instruments in this culture being music, poetry and art.[20] On my reading of Mill, then, a person would be said to display his individuality in 'outward' activity, in discussion and in "various modes of action", i.e. in situations where what he does may directly affect others adversely and so require the imposition of social controls.[21] The cultivation of his susceptibilities would be a vital element in the self-development of any such person, but unlike his individuality it would not directly issue in outward action and so would not provoke the question: "How much of human life should be assigned to individuality, and how much to society?"[22]

---

[19] See e.g. OL, pp.68, 114, 116, 118, 127, 133.
[20] See *Autobiography, op.cit.,* pp.100-106.
[21] cf. OL, pp.68-9, 114-5, 131-2.
[22] *Ibid.,* p.131.

Finally, I draw attention to the fact that my reading of Mill's view of individuality can comfortably accommodate the two passages, quoted above, in which Mill might seem to be equating individuality with self-development. For, on closer inspection, it is clear that both passages are quite compatible with my interpretation of individuality as being the primary, indispensable condition of and also the most important part of self-development. That this interpretation is more likely to be the correct one is confirmed when we turn to a number of crucial passages in which Mill explains the connection between individuality and self-perfection. But first let me glance at Mill's discussion of the free will problem.

Self-Determination and Free Will

We have seen that what Benthamite psychological theory lacked was the conception of a free and rational will capable of making its own choices. A man could come to act, Mill argued, not out of regard for his own private interest but out of a desire to be a better sort of person, to improve his own character and to do good for others. In the course of arriving at the view that self-determination or the capacity for choice is a necessary condition for achieving the best and happiest life Mill became oppressed by the problem of free will. His problem was one of somehow reconciling his by now deeply held belief in self-determination as a precondition of self-development with his long-standing commitment to the doctrine of philosophical necessity, a doctrine which appeared to make the individual a mere victim of external circumstances. A way out of his dilemma occurred to Mill when he perceived that "though our character is formed by circumstances, our own desires can do much to shape those circumstances; and that what is really inspiriting and ennobling in the doctrine of freewill, is the conviction that we have real power over the formation of our own character; that our will, by influencing some of our circumstances, can modify our future habits or capabilities of willing."[23]

The desire to amend our own character, Mill is saying, can itself become a strong and independent motive. Hence, insofar as they issue

---

[23] *Autobiography, op.cit.,* p.119; cf. *Logic, op.cit.* Book VI, ch.II, sec.3.

from this desire our actions, while in accordance with the law of causality, may nevertheless correctly be said to be *our* actions, to be due to ourselves and not merely the outcome of external circumstances. As an answer to the problem of the freedom of the will, Mill's solution may not be satisfactory. Its difficulties need not, however, give us pause; its relevance to my argument lies only in its connection with Mill's doctrine of self-development. Since self-development is, in the main, a process of self-activity, Mill could see he had to face up to the philosophical problem of the freedom of the will before he could go on to vindicate the place of self-determination in the achievement of the good life.

Individuality and Self-Development

It is not acting or expressing an opinion as such that develops a man. For a man to do these things out of conformity is not, Mill believes, to "educate or develop in him any of the qualities which are the distinctive endowment of a human being". He writes:

> "The human faculties of perception, judgment, discriminative feeling, mental activity, and even moral preference, are exercised only in making a choice. He who does anything because it is the custom makes no choice. He gains no practice either in discerning or in desiring what is best. The mental and moral, like the muscular powers, are improved only by being used. The faculties are called into no exercise by doing a thing merely because others do it, no more than by believing a thing only because others believe it. If the grounds of an opinion are not conclusive to the person's own reason, his reason cannot be strengthened, but is likely to be weakened, by his adopting it: and if the inducements to an act are not such as are consentaneous to his own feelings and character (where affection, or the rights of others are not concerned) it is so much done towards rendering his feelings and character inert and torpid, instead of active and energetic."[24]

He then makes a contrast. On the one hand there is the man who "lets the world, or his own portion of it, choose his plan of life for him" and who "has no need of any other faculty than the ape-like one of imitation". On the other hand there is the man with a considerable capacity for choice:

> "He who chooses his plan for himself, employs all his faculties. He must use observation to see, reasoning and

---
[24] OL, pp.116-17.

judgment to foresee, activity to gather materials for decision, discrimination to decide, and when he has decided, firmness and self-control to hold to his deliberate decision. And these qualities he requires and exercises exactly in proportion as the part of his conduct which he determines according to his own judgment and feelings is a large one."[25]

Further evidence that self-determination is the principal condition of self-perfection is to be found in Chapter II of the *Liberty*. Here most of the space is given to justifying freedom of thought and discussion on the grounds that it is a prerequisite if the best thinkers are to have the opportunity of arriving at rational and true belief and promoting social progress. But Mill does not defend freedom of thought and discussion solely on these grounds. "On the contrary", he says, "it is as *much and even more indispensable* to enable *average human beings* to attain the mental stature which they are capable of ".[26] He believes, with the Protestants, that "the intellect and judgment of mankind ought to be cultivated" - not merely, that is, as a means of arriving at true knowledge but because intellectual understanding is a desirable object in itself. And he goes on to say that if "the cultivation of the understanding consists in one thing more than in another, it is surely in learning the grounds of one's own opinions".[27]

Just as the strength of a muscle is developed by using it to exert force and its developed strength consists in its capacity to exert force, so individuality, or self-determination, Mill believes, is both the chief means of achieving self-development and the chief component of th developed self. Society and the state may either aid or hinder the process, but the growth of individuality depends mainly on people giving free play to their own "inward forces", depends, in other words, on the active and continuous employment of their own higher capacities. It is, then, in independent activity, in thinking for themselves, making their own moral decisions, that individuals come first to discover and then to strengthen and display their own distinctive abilities in one or more of these areas. Men are made human (become individuals or realise themselves) largely by their capacity for self-determination. If a man's thoughts and actions are determined, not by "his

---

[25] *Ibid.,* p.117.
[26] *Ibid.,* p.94. My italics.
[27] *Ibid.,* p.96.

own judgment and feelings", but by intimidation, or if he habitually obeys the dictates of custom or public opinion, his faculties are not called into play and so are rendered passive and torpid. The "human faculties" of such men become "withered and starved", they cease to have any opinions or feelings which can properly be called their own, and they no longer have any character. "Now is this, or is it not", Mill asks, "the desirable condition of human nature?"[28]

In clarifying Mill's conception of man I have stressed that self-direction assumes a very special or preferred position. Self-determination is always of supreme value because only through the exercise of self-determination can men hope to become fully human. Much (though not all) human excellence can only be attained by activity or effort; the 'active' faculties are improved only when they are used and they are used only in judging and choosing. The very formation of personality, the very possibility of each individual's coming to acquire his own determinate and distinctive set of inellectual, moral and emotional capacities requires his being able to think and act according to his own judgment and inclinations.

The man Mill most admired is the man who is intellectually active, whose desires are vigorous and whose will is strong, and who thereby stands apart from ordinary men. What Mill cared for most was enterprising men, men of outstanding intellect and energetic character, who were ever grappling with new ideas and experimenting with new ways of living. Thus self-determination emerges as the most vital of man's essential interests. Even though his criticism of their doctrine and its implications had an undertow of confusion and hesitation, Mill was successful in widening the earlier liberal theory of motive by drawing attention to men's need or potentiality for freedom, or individuality - one of the permanent interests of man of which Benthamite liberalism had taken very little account. A basic presupposition of Mill's liberalism is a certain conception or definition of man: to say of someone that he is a man is to say that he has some need and potential capacity for rational self-direction; and that freedom, in this sense is not merely a condition of his self-development but is also a large and vital ingredient of his developed self.

---

[28]*Ibid.*, pp.116-120.

Self-Development
as The Ultimate End

In the course of his crucial seven-page discussion early in Chapter III of *On Liberty* [29] Mill lays down what is an unmistakeably Aristotelian account of the good life and virtually abandons the orthodox Utilitarian account of the ultimate end. Having commended von Humboldt's doctrine, he elaborates his own view of self-development, then closes this part of his argument by first declaring "that it is only the cultivation of individuality which produces, or can produce, well-developed human beings", and then asking: "what more or better can be said of any condition of human affairs than that it brings human beings themselves nearer to the best thing they can be?"[30] Mill appeals specifically to the "Greek ideal of self-development", and throughout these early pages of Chapter III can be seen relying upon the Greek doctrine of function as a vindication of the good life for man. He is committing himself to the view that to say of a man that he is good is simply to say that he is perfect, properly developed as a *man,* that he is an admirable example of the species 'man': "Among the works of man, which human life is rightly employed in perfecting and beautifying, the first in importance surely is man himself".[31] And again he writes: "Human nature is not a machine to be built after a model. . . . . but a tree, which requires to grow and develop itself on all sides, according to the tendency of the inward forces which make it a living thing".[32] In these and other passages in this part of Chapter III Mill is presupposing that there is involved in the very definition of man a conception of his characteristic end or purpose. The same self-realization doctrine also emerges in an *ad hominem* type argument used in criticising Calvinism when Mill says those who believe men to have been made by a good God must surely believe that such a Being "gave all human faculties that they might be cultivated and unfolded. . . . and that he takes delight in every nearer approach made by his creatures to the ideal conception embodied in them, every increase in any of their capabilities of comprehension, of action, or of enjoyment ". In so far as they cultivate and call forth "the ideal conception embodied in

---

[29] *Ibid.,* pp.115-21.
[30] *Ibid.,* p.121.
[31] *Ibid.,* p.117.
[32] *Ibid.,* p.117.

them" by cultivating what is individual in themselves, human beings become more valuable both to themselves and to others.[33]

Mill is here following Aristotle in claiming man possesses certain essential powers distinguishing him from other animals and requiring from their very nature to be developed. There are, he thinks, certain "qualities which are the distinctive endowment of a human being", namely the "human faculties of perception, judgment, discriminative feeling, mental activity, and moral preference. . . ."[34] Each type of thing or animal (it is assumed) has its own characteristic activity or purpose marking it off from other things and constituting its peculiar excellence. The value of any particular instance of the type is guaged by the degree to which it is a good example of that type. What distinguishes man from other animals is his possession of the specifically "human faculties, capacities and susceptibilities". And since the goodness of everything, it is assumed, consists in developing its peculiar characteristics, the good of man lies in the cultivation of his characteristically human powers, his "noble" or "higher" capacities.

---

[33] *Ibid.*, p.121.
[34] *Ibid.*, p.116.

CHAPTER VI

FALLIBILISM, INDIVIDUALITY
and
THE OPENNESS OF HUMAN NATURE

My account of Mill's liberalism so far has focussed mainly on the interlocking notions of happiness, self-development, and individuality (or self-determination), notions which together make up the greater part of his conception of man. And his conception of man may itself be seen as the most important component of what I earlier decribed as the philosophical level of Mill's liberalism. But as well as presupposing a certain view of the nature of man, Mill's liberalism rests on a fallibilist view of the nature and possibilities of human knowledge. This, too is an aspect of his thought at the more philosophical level which enters into and becomes a fundamental component of his liberalism. What is more, Mill's fallibilism will also be seen to have a significant influence on his concept of man, issuing in a view of human nature as essentially open or incomplete.

Liberalism and Fallibilism

Mill is an empiricist in grounding all knowledge on experience; he believes that nothing can be established as being true except on the evidence of our senses. Moreover, it is always possible in principle for new observations to upset old conclusions, over-turning theories which we imagined to be well-established. Human knowledge is alway fallible and alway incomplete; hence we can never claim certainty for any theory or doctrine, but we may hold most firmly to those hypotheses which have been given the best opportunity of being questioned. "The beliefs which we have most warrant for", says Mill, "have no safeguard to rest on, but a standing invitation to the whole world to prove them unfounded".[1] If the quest for absolute certainty is fruitless even in natural philosophy, how much more is it likely to be so in human affairs, and how much more necessary is it

---
[1] *Ibid.*, p.83.

therefore that any and every doctrine be allowed the possibility of refutation. When we turn to "morals, religion, politics, social relations, and the business of life, three-fourths of the arguments for every disputed opinion consist in dispelling the appearances which favour some opinion different from it".[2]

This very general theoretical belief concerning the nature and possilbility of our knowledge is one basis of Mill's doctrine of toleration, which is a vital element in his liberalism. If in the ideological sphere it is especially true that uncertainty reigns, then unless toleration of all doctrines and practices (short of definite injury to others) is allowed, we cannot ever hope to arrive at true opinions or discover which are the best ways of life. So Mill writes:

> "That mankind are not infallible; that their truths, for the most part, are only half-truths; that unity of opinion, unless resulting from the fullest and freest comparison of opposite opinions, is not desirable, and diversity not an evil, but a good, until mankind are much more capable than at present of recognising all sides of the truth, are principles applicable to men's modes of action, not less than their opinions.
>
> As it is useful that while mankind are imperfect there should be different opinions, so it is that there should be different experiments of living; that free scope should be given to varieties of character, short of injury to others; and that the worth of different modes of life should be proved practically, when any one thinks fit to try them."[3]

Mill's thesis is that men are fallible and imperfect at present (and will be as far as we can see into the future). We, therefore, cannot be sure that any doctrine is not a source of truth nor any way of living a source of goodness. Hence we must allow men and women free scope to discuss diverse views and to try out various "experiments of living". Unless we do this, many at present unforeseeable opinions and forms of human fulfilment will be left untried and we shall never know whether they are true or worthwhile. Mill is very deeply committed to the belief that we can never be sure until we have tested them whether opinions are worth subscribing to or ways of life worth following.

---

[2] *Ibid.,* p.96.
[3] *Ibid.,* p.115.

Mill's doctrine of the fallibility of human knowledge also carries with it an asumption concerning the nature of man: it is assumed that human nature is essentially indeterminate and incomplete, that it is left open for indefinite development. Man himself has the continuous capacity for free choice and experiment and since he is fallible there is an unpredictable element in human nature; man's nature is, in principle, left open for development in many different and unknown directions. On this assumption, we can never know in advance what may be the motives and needs of the men and women of some future era. Though Mill himself has been dead less than a hundred years, Englishmen seem already to have adopted some very different general beliefs about the ways of living they think their nature demands. However, this may be, given the increasing rate of social change in our own era, we assuredly are not going to be able to anticipate what may be among the most fundamental moral ideas and attitudes of those living a hundred years from now.

Since openness is an integral part of Mill's concept of the individual it further follows that opaqueness is also to be regarded as a necessary part of man's nature. Our knowledge of everything, including persons, is necessarily incomplete. Furthermore, since human beings are all in some degree self-determining, this again means there will always be something unfathomable or impenetrable about each individual. Or putting the same point another way, one may take Mill to be saying that no individual is ever completely definable, so that the concept of man carries with it what might be called the notion of partial indefinability. This way of looking at men and women provides Mill with a powerful argument for an initial presumption in favour of toleration; if we know we can never fully understand other people we do well to suspend judgment, to adopt a 'wait and see attitude'. Such a stance is implacably opposed to that of the fanatical moralist who, convinced that on the subject of human nature he has all the answers, is only too ready to impose his 'solutions' on other people. To follow up this question now would, however, distract me from my task of trying to bring out the manner in which Mill's fallibilism functions as one of the basic elements of his liberalism. Something more will be said concerning Mill's case for toleration in Part II when I come to consider the various formulations of his well-known principle of self-protection. My task in the remainder of this chapter is to explore further the way in which the fallibilist strain in Mill's thinking is related to his concept of man.

Individuality and the
Openness of Human Nature

Two presuppositions of Mill's liberalism may easily be taken to be discordant: I speak of his fallibilism and his doctrine of individuality. How, it might be asked, can a liberalism formulated partly in terms of fallibilism and the essential openness and uncertainty of human nature leave any room for the view that men and women may be said to possess personal identity or individuality? If our account of Mill's model of man is correct, it now seems to shelter a fatal inconsistency. On the one hand, the notions of self-development and individuality seem essentially to postulate for each man a determinate personal identity, a distinctive configuration of characteristics and powers giving him some measure of independence of his social milieu and environment generally. On the other hand, the notion of individuality (self-determination) involves, as I have said, notions of openness and indeterminacy which apparently forbid us to conceive of the individual as definable in terms of any unchanging characteristics, oblige us to treat a man's individuality as being somehow a matter of his indefinability. Does this seeming contradiction mean there is an incoherence right at the very centre of Mill's liberalism? I believe not. Let us now see how the apparent dilemma may be resolved.

The problem is hinted at but left on one side by Sir Isiah Berlin in the course of tracing some of the implications of Mill's adherence to fallibilism. From fallibilism it follows that men are altered by discovering new truths and trying out new experiences so that, Berlin argues:
> "the notion common to Aristotelians, and Christian scholastics and atheistical materialists alike, that there exists a basic knowable human nature, one and the same, at all times, in all places, in all men - a static, unchanging substance underneath the altering appearances, with permanent needs, dictated by a single, knowable goal, the same for all mankind, is mistaken..."[4]

Berlin is correct in suggesting that Mill's view of man amounts to a break with the picture of a determined and static human nature and the

---
[4] Sir Isiah Berlin, *John Stuart Mill and The Ends of LIfe*, (London, 1959) p.17.

substitution for it of a conception of human nature as free to "expand itself in innumerable and conflicting directions".[5] The picture of man inherited by Mill from his liberal predecessors did indeed tacitly assume that there is such a thing as a comparatively simple and unalterable human nature, completely formed and fully ascertainable. Commenting on Bentham's theory of human life, Mill concludes that "Man, that most complex being, is a very simple one in his eyes".[6] And in place of the Benthamite image of man, with its crude and over-confident hedonism, its assumption that human nature is definable by a few unchanging characteristics, Mill proceeded to build up a more complex and open-ended picture. Furthermore, for the reasons he advances, it also looks as if there will necessarily always be something uncertain and unfathomable about every individual. Besides, much of the zest and interest in human life arises out of our discovering and rediscovering that the conduct and experience of human beings is not congealed in some ahistorical state, that it changes (sometimes dramatically, more often gradually) over time, so that in a modern industrial society especially, human nature may alter quite markedly over a period of a hundred years or less. Mill's amendment of the earlier liberal tradition so as to take into account this aspect of human nature is therefore to be welcomed.

But this part of Mill's account of human nature assuredly is incompatible with what Berlin describes as the classical model of man, the conception of man's personality as something fully understandable, fixed and certain. If we believe, with Mill, that uncertainty of nature is part of our notion of the individual we cannot continue to support Aristotle's assumption that we are somehow given complete and final insight into the true nature of man. Yet whilst Mill's empiricist-derived insistence that uncertainty of human nature is part of our concept of an individual remains incompatible with the *classical* account of man, it is not for that reason in conflict with *his own* view that man is, in part, definable by his possession of the distinctively human powers of mind, feeling and moral judgment. For the truth is that we need not, as Aristotle did, think of such powers as being absolutely fixed and unalterable. We can, while retaining the notion of the human species possessing certain essential powers, distinguish between those powers, and their particular form of expression within a given

---

[5] *Autobiography, op,cit.,* p.177.
[6] "Bentham", *op.cit.,* p.101.

historical culture; in so doing room may be left within Mill's concept of human nature for the notion of contingency. It is not being suggested for a moment that this was Mill's own solution to the difficulty we have raised. There is, indeed no evidence for his ever being aware of the need to try to reconcile the two apparently discordant elements in his picture of man. Still, the problem is one which his account of man's essential powers is required to meet, so there is some point in following up my proposed way of overcoming it.

Stuart Hampshire, when speaking of such persisting ideas of human excellence as friendship and justice, draws an important distinction between these relatively unchanging abstract ideals and the criteria by which men in different periods and cultures have in practice characterised them. He writes:

> "A common centre of meaning, and common conditions in the criteria, persist with the persisting idea of that which is distinctively human. But the more specific conditions in the criteria of application of such terms as justice and friendship change, as the conditions of social life in which they are applied change".[7]

Mill's model of man may be looked at once again, this time in the light of Hampshire's observation. Central in Mill's conception of the good man, is his individuality, his capacity for choice; and, in the modern European context anyway, it scarcely seems possible that this intellectual-cum-moral capacity shoud ever be thought of as irrelevant in a consideration of what are the distinctive human endowments. The same thing might be said of those emotional and aesthetic powers which, for Mill, go to make up the personality of the good man; these also are among the relatively unchanging characteristics of man. If this is so, then it would look as if man may, in part, be defined by the possession of what are at least *relatively unchanging* characteristics. Nevertheless, while there are, in this sense, certain more or less permanent human powers which are part of the concept of man, the particular ways of thinking, feeling and acting - the various modes of character that are thought to give *expression* to or *embody* these aspects of human excellence - do in fact change quite markedly over time. It is the existence of these latter, relatively impermanent and inessential forms of behaviour, in which the changing ideals of self-perfection are incorporated, that enables us to speak of the

---

[7] Stuart Hampshire, *Thought and Action* (London, 1960) pp.247-8.

partial indefinability of human nature and so leave room in our concept of man for the idea of his openness and opaqueness.

The point may be elaborated and brought out more sharply if we consider the value Mill accords to the ideal of self-determination or individuality. Whether or not we accept his evaluation of it as the most important of the essential human interests, we should probably agree that freedom, understood in this very general or abstract sense, has been for a quite considerable time an important constituent in the liberal conception of man. It is doubtful, however, whether men and women in a free society care very much for self-determination merely *as such*. What many do in practice seem to value are rather various forms of activity or ways of life which, as it were, instantiate the abstract freedom of self-determination. For freedom as self-determination may (even within the one European society and at the one time) assume a variety of different forms or modes of expression. Consider, for instance, Mill's insistence on the value of participation in public life as a way of engaging and cultivating man's capacities for reasonable judgment and deliberate choice. Men and women who do manage to be active in social affairs might be said to be allowing their powers of self-direction a particular avenue of expression, or to be embodying them in a concrete way of life. For them, taking an active share in conducting the common affairs of the community *is* a form of self-determination, a mode of living that enables their individuality to flower; they do not feel free (and are not free) unless they are exercising their 'political' freedom. On the other hand, there may be other members of the same community who, while feeling the need to think and act for themselves, set little store upon the participation in community affairs as a vehicle for the display and cultivation of their freedom. They may, for instance, find more scope for the realization of their active powers in the part of their lives given over to business, to the following of some profession or to the carrying on of an artistic pursuit.

It is in acting within the context of their various social roles or spheres of activity that individuals may be said to exercise and develop their powers of self-determination. And it is not the abstract power of self-determination but the exercise of their own intitiative within a special area of activity that they come to care for and to value. Mill was well aware that the ways of life of many men and even more women provide few opportunities for the display of this sort of freedom. What may be called the institutional structure of his liberalism is a fairly sustained effort to sketch, in institutional terms, the kind of society which would be required in order to provide the necessary setting for his ideal individual. No doubt, in making this attempt, he failed to consider carefully and systematically enough some of the difficult problems. No doubt he omitted to take fully into account the complexity of the considerations to be dealt with in sketching the kind of political and social system within and by which the free life is to be realized and maintained. If I may pause to comment on one element in his outline of a liberal society, I should say he seems to have been altogether too optimistic in thinking that the majority of citizens in democratic nations would come to see participation in political and private associations as an important avenue for the expression and perfecting of their active powers. Yet even here it is necessary to sound a note of caution. The notion of polticial participation is once again becoming a live political issue, and we certainly cannot foresee with any accuracy what role it may come to play in the future.

CHAPTER VII

THE JUSTIFICATION OF LIBERALISM

John Stuart Mill's philosophy of politics is, in broad terms, an effort to elaborate the good life for man and to fill out a picture of the social and political arrangements which would best enable that life to be realised. And moreover, that philosophy takes its departure, as I have been suggesting, from certain fundamental beliefs about man and society, so that the kind of social and political structure Mill thinks possible and desirable depends in part on the mental, moral and other powers he attributes to man. So far my aim has been to bring to the surface the particular conception of man which lies at the foundation of Mill's liberalism. My thesis has been that he can be shown as singling out man's potentiality for individual self-development through the exercise of individuality as the prime distinguishing characteristic and highest excellence of man.

The Justification of Liberalism

Many English and American philosophers would contend there is no possiblity of deriving a view of the good life for man from a belief about the nature of man. If Mill's liberalism is based on the view that the good life ought to consist in the perfection of our higher capacities then what authority, it will be asked, can possibly lie behind this 'ought'? Has not Hume shown that we cannot derive an 'ought' from an 'is'? So that even supposing we were somehow able to establish by empirical investigation that all men do have a central need and potentiality for self-development in Mill's sense, no conclusions would follow concerning whether or not that need or potentiality ought to be fulfilled.

J.C. Rees, who wishes to reserve an important place for practical philosophy in political thinking, has suggested a way out of this difficulty. He concedes the force of standard objections to a naturalistic form of justification but goes on to argue for a weaker, hence more defensible sense of 'justification'. Agreeing with those who contend that the principles of a philosophy of politics cannot possibly be derived from axioms relating to the nature of man, Rees nevertheless thinks the political theorist does not have far to tread before finding firm ground underfoot. Rees argues that although the practical political philosopher cannot appeal to ultimate foundations, he does not need to set about the elaboration of a normative philosophy of politics in a quite arbitrary way - by trying, perhaps, to conjure a body of moral and political criteria out of the air. Criteria are "already to hand in the society around him in the shape of those moral principles and standards which he employs as a private person or as a citizen, both in the normal routine of living and on rare occasions of acute moral perplexity."[1] Applying this to liberalism, Rees would presumably say that the liberal thinker could take his departure from the liberal tradition itself, by considering the moral and political criteria worked out by past and present liberal thinkers and in some measure exemplified in the social and political life of his own society.[2]

A too casual acquaintance with Mill's writings might lead us to suppose not merely that he would have agreed with Rees but also that his own method of justifying liberalism exemplifies that recommended by Rees. Of course Mill did inherit the liberal tradition formulated by the earlier Philosophical Radicals and, in a sense, his own liberalism does take its departure from that tradition. What is more, Mill might possibly have agreed with Rees's contention that most everyday political issues are concerned with the disputed application of *given or accepted* political principles to concrete situations. But, as a moral and political philosopher, he could scarcely have accepted a view which would have denied him the possibility of going beyond the specific principles to be found either in the liberal tradition or embodied in a particular society and attempting to justify them by appealing to beliefs of a more ultimate character. He would not have been satisfied with a method of justification whereby we justify a particular principle simply by showing it to be linked with other principles held by members of the same tradition or society. For he recognized that there are, as a matter of fact, conflicting traditions and ways of life even within a single society (not to mention differences between societies) and the thoughtful person may sometimes find himself called upon to offer an ultimate

---

[1] J.C. Rees, "The Limitations of Political Theory", *Political Studies,* Vol.2, No.3, p.256.

[2] Such also seems to be the view of P.H. Partridge as expressed in *Thinking About Politics, op.cit.,* p.19.

justification of one of his more fundmental political principles. In so doing he necessarily commits himself to the validity of a *theory of ethical justification* which consistency would oblige him to defend against its rivals.

Mill was especially concerned to defend a naturalistic form of ethical justification against what he regarded as the arbitrary dogmatism of "Intuitionism", represented by the then dominant philosophical schools of German idealism and common sense philosophy. He was opposed to intuitionism not simply on logical and epistemological grounds but also because he saw it as a towering philosophical obstacle standing in the path of individual and social progress. In his *Autobiography* he contrasts Intuitionism with his own philosophy of Experience: "the difference between these two schools of philosophy, that of Intuition, and that of Experience and Association, is not a mere matter of abstract speculation; it is full of practical consequences, and lies at the foundation of all the greatest differences of practical opinion in an age of progress".[3] Intuitionism, Mill had declared earlier in his *Autobiography,* is "the greatest intellectual support of false doctrines and bad institutions" because by its aid "every inveterate belief and every intense feeling. . . is enabled to dispense with the obligation of justifying itself by reason, and is erected into its own all-sufficient voucher and justification".[4] Mill thought intuitionism had an especially damaging influence in the sphere of social morality, reinforcing the "tyranny" of popular prejudice by conferring upon it a pseudo-philosophical respectability. The inveterate opponents of human progress relied most heavily upon an appeal to intuitive truths, to custom and authority. Hence in order to achieve any success, the liberal reformer must be able to work out a scientific philosophy of experience which would expose the ultimate irrationality of all such appeals.

To canvass even the most important of Mill's arguments against the intuitionist school would be well beyond the scope of my project. It is enough to note that, for Mill, the crucial flaw in intuitionist ethical theory was its failure to provide any rational basis for either the discussion or the amendment of moral beliefs. My interest, though, is in Mill's effort to formulate a naturalistic ethic which would be a scientifically based alternative to intuitionism. I am concerned with his attempt to justify his

---
[3] *Autobiography, op.cit.,* pp.191-92.
[4] *Ibid.,* p.158.

ultimate moral principle, thus providing a sound foundation for his liberalism. On the one hand, Mill seeks to avoid the, as he believes, dogmatic and arbitrary intuitionist appeal to our moral sense as the source of moral knowledge. He wishes to argue that though a fundamental moral doctrine is incapable of strict proof, it does not follow that "its acceptance or rejection must depend on blind impulse, or arbitrary choice."[5] And he thinks reasons can be adduced for our preferring one value system to another. Accordingly, he looks to some type of naturalistic or quasi-scientific foundation for ultimate moral principles. Yet he had also read his Hume, and is so far from being committed to the belief that a descriptive statement may strictly entail a value judgment that he goes to greater pains than does Hume to insist on the ineradicable distinction between statements of fact and statements of value. The question Mill raises here is so crucial for his liberalism that it must be examined at greater length.

Fact, Value and Moral Individualism

Before embarking upon a detailed examination of Mill's justification of liberalism it will be as well to point out a vital respect in which that justification is related to his moral individualism. According to Mill, any attempt to build a safe logical bridge between statements of fact and statements of value is bound to be fallacious. He might equally well have observed that the very attempt to construct such a bridge runs directly counter to his own individualist ethic. Closely associated with and required by the outlook of moral individualism is what has now come to be called the doctrine of the autonomy of morals - with its requirement of there being no possibility of bridging the gap between fact and value. Any individual engaged in moral activity will always be able to give reasons to others (and to himself) for what he believes or does. Such reasons may be other moral principles and may also concern the facts of the situation. But since he has ultimately to make up his own mind concerning his moral commitments there must come an end to the giving of reasons: unless his evaluations flow, in the last resort, from his own free and deliberate *decision* they will not be true or genuine moral evaluations. From the requirement that if

---

[5] U, p.4.

individuals are to be moral they must, in the end, *choose* their own intellectual and moral commitments, it follows that genuine moral evaluations cannot be forced upon them by the mere *recognition* of facts concerning the nature of man or of society. If this were possible, if, as Alan Montefiore has expressed it, "a recognition of facts were ever to carry an entailed commitment to any sort of approval or evaluation, the individual would have lost his unconditioned freedom to determine his values on the basis of personal decision alone".[6]

In short, to give up the ultimate distinction between fact and value would be to take the act of choice out of the moral life; it would be to abandon moral individualism and with it the fundamental presupposition of liberalism. It would seem, therefore, that the possibility of sustaining a liberal philosophy of politics depends upon denying that facts about man and society can ever strictly entail moral principles. If this is so, how can one reconcile Mill's moral individualism with his belief that it does, nevertheless, *in some sense,* remain possible to justify liberalism by an appeal to empirical evidence concerning the nature of man? In order to answer that question we shall now have to turn (as was promised earlier) to a detailed consideration of what Mill has to say concerning the logic of the relationship between fact and value. For Mill has frequently been accused of believing it possible to derive fundamental moral principles logically from empirical propositions about the nature of man. If this interpretation could be upheld, then Mill's meta-ethics would certainly be inconsistent with his moral individualism. But as I hope to show, such an interpretation involves a serious misunderstanding of Mill's position.

On the Distinction Between
Art and Science

Mill has often been accused of trying to derive the conclusion that happiness alone is desirable logically from man's supposedly universal desire for happiness. This interpretation of Mill is open to at least two

---
[6] A. Montefiore, "Fact, Value and Ideology", in B. Williams and A. Montefiore (eds.) *British Analytical Philosophy* (London, 1966) pp.198-9. Italics in original.

serious objections. First, Mill explicitly rejects as logically incoherent any such simple form of ethical naturalism. Secondly, his actual proof of the principle of utility is not intended as a strict logical proof. Let us first consider his views on the problem of the fact-value distinction. Having done that we shall examine the argument he gives in support of his first principle.

In his essay 'Nature' Mill suggests his general position concerning the naturalistic fallacy. "All inquiries", he says, "are either into what is, or into what ought to be: science and history belonging to the first division, art, morals and politics to the second".[7] But his view of how the ultimate principles of an ethical system are related to empirical knowledge is most fully set out in the final chapter of *A System of Logic* and in Chapters I and IV of *Utilitarianism*. Turning first to the chapter in the *Logic* entitled "Of the Logic of Practice, or Art; including Morality or Policy", we find Mill describing ethics, or morality, as being a branch of the Art of Life. There is, he emphasizes, a clear-cut distinction to be drawn between the methods of Art and those of Science. The moral sciences (what would now be called the social sciences) are concerned with inquires into "the course of nature" and are to be distinguished from an "inquiry the results of which do not express themselves in the indicative, but in the imperative mood".[8] Propositions which define the end of an art (the propositions of morality are among these) are not propositions of science: "Propositions of science assert a matter of fact. . . The propositions now spoken of [i.e. those of art, including morality] do not assert that anything is, but enjoin or recommend that something should be. They are a class by themselves. A proposition of which the predicate is expressed by the words *ought or should be,* is generically different from one which is expressed by *is* or *will be* ."[9] While thus stressing the sharp distinction between descriptive and normative inquiries, Mill allows that the moralist is nevertheless dependent upon the scientist in this respect: morality proposes to itself a goal to be aimed at; it then defines this end and hands back over to science; science having explored what causes and conditions secure the goal hands back to morality a theorem which sets out the combination of circumstances by

---

[7] 'Nature', in G. Nakhnikian (ed.) *John Stuart Mill, Nature and Utility of Religion* (New York, 1958) p.9.
[8] J.S. Mill, *A System of Logic, op.cit.,* p.616.
[9] *Ibid,* pp.619-20. Italics in original.

which the end could be produced. Morality then examines these circumstances, and, if it has been told that the performance of certain actions will attain the end, may conclude that their performance is desirable. But even though the scientist can in this manner supply to the moralist factual information showing that certain results flow from certain causes and that to attain particular goals certain means are the most appropriate, it is no part of his role as a scientist to pronounce on whether or not such goals ought to be pursued. For although "the reasonings which connect the end or purpose of every art with its means belong to the domain of Science, the definition of the end itself belongs exlusively to Art, and forms its peculiar province. Every art has one first principle, or general major premise, not borrowed from science; that which enunciates the object aimed at, and affirms it to be a desirable object."[10] Mill is here affirming very plainly that every morality possesses at least one first principle, expressed in a normative proposition. He certainly does claim to be able to deduce significant ethical conclusions from this major premise, but this is only because it is itself normative or, to reiterate Mill's words, "enunciates the object aimed at and affirms it to be a desirable object ".

When we turn to his *Utilitarianism* we find Mill once again stressing the need to avoid the naturalistic fallacy. The principle he is striving to vindicate in Chapter IV of *Utilitarianism* is that happiness is the only thing desirable as an end. Again it is clear that he does not look upon this as any kind of descriptive or scientific statement. Morality, he informs us, is a "practical art" and its "rules of action" provide us with guidance for the conduct of life.[11] In the opening remarks to the chapter he compares the first principles of our knowledge with those of our conduct, maintaining that the former are matters of fact and implying that ultimate practical principles are not. Moreover, the latter are never susceptible of proof in the ordinary meaning of that term: "Questions of ultimate ends are not amenable to direct proof. Whatever can be proved to be good, must be so by being shown to be a means to something admitted to be good without proof ".[12] It would seem that whatever Mill was trying to do in Chapter IV of *Utilitarianism* he was *not purporting* to prove a first principle of morals by deducing it from a descriptive statement.

---

[10] *Logic, op.cit.,* p.619.
[11] U, pp.2, 11.
[12] *Ibid.,* p.4, and cf. pp.32-33.

Aristotelianism and Justification

Mill, then, consistently maintained the impossibility of validly deducing ethical conclusions from purely factual premises and this is what we should expect from a writer deeply committed to moral individualism. Yet he still thought it possible to find some kind of naturalistic foundation for ultimate moral principles. As I emphasized in Chapter IV, he relies heavily on an Aristotelian-type ethical naturalism. His liberalism presupppposes an Aristotelian conception of man according to which it is somehow incumbent on men and women to develop their peculiarly human potentialities.

In invoking the Aristotelian concept of *nature* Mill is relying upon the teleological sense of 'nature'. In this teleological sense, every type of thing or species has its own nature (or end); its characteristic excellence is realized in doing that which brings about the realization of this end. Thus man is conceived of as aiming towards a definite optimum condition of perfection which is the specific good appropriate to him. This teleological mode of thinking may, as H.L.A. Hart has noted, seem odd when stated abstractly.[13] Still, it does in some ways accord with the manner in which we think and speak about living things, including human beings. Just as it is in the nature of an acorn to become an oak tree, so it is in man's nature to develop his human capacities. "Human nature", Mill wrote, is like "a tree, which requires to grow and develop itself on all sides according to the tendency of the inward forces which make it a living thing".[14] In this and in other passages Mill is operating with a notion of the normal or proper development of man and of the needs he is required to satisfy for that development.

Now, this teleological notion of nature swallows up the customary distinction between evaluation and description - upon which Mill in other places insists. For on this view human nature is conceived of as containing in itself levels of excellence which human beings strive to realize. As Hart puts it: "on the teleological view, the events regularly befalling things are not thought of *merely* as occurring regularly, and the questions whether

---

[13] H.L.A. Hart, The Concept of Law (Oxford, 1963) p.185.
[14] OL, p.117.

they *do* occur or whether they *should* occur or whether it is *good* that they occur are not regarded as separate questions. On the contrary, ... what generally occurs can both be explained and evaluated as good or what ought to occur, by exhibiting it as a step towards the proper end or good of the thing concerned. The laws of a thing's development therefore show both how it should and how it does regularly behave or change".[15] In this sense of 'nature', in which the nature of a thing consists in the characteristic excellence which it is capable of attaining, the end at which man aims is *necessarily* good. The development of his higher capacities is not man's good because he desires it; rather he desires it simply because it is already, or antecedently, his own proper end or good.

Mill, however, is unable to accept the functionalist assumption that since man differs from animals in possessing higher capacities, which he aims to develop, this in itself somehow constitutes the only 'reason' that can be given for justifying their development. To have accepted that position would have been incompatible with his view of the disjunction between fact and value and inconsonant with his moral individualism. Such a simple form of naturalism is rejected by Mill in his essay, "Nature". There he states that even though the "artificially perfected nature of the best and noblest human beings is the only nature which it is ever commendable to follow", it is necessary to add that "even this cannot be erected into a standard of conduct, since it is itself the fruit of training and culture the choice of which, if rational and not accidental, must have been determined by a standard already chosen".[16] Thus Mill reveals himself to be aware that a naturalistic doctrine of functionalist justification is acceptable only if one first covertly assumes some such principle as that man ought to develop his distinctively human nature. And in *Utilitarianism* the problem, as he sees it, becomes one of showing how such a principle is itself to be justified.

The 'Proof' of an Ultimate End

Mill's problem in Chapter IV of *Utilitarianism* is to escape the charge that his own ethical doctrine is no more capable of rational defence than the

---

[15] Hart, *op.cit.,* p.185. Italics in original.
[16] "Nature", *op.cit.,* p.37.

much maligned intuitionism; but without, in so doing, committing the naturalistic fallacy. Though the utilitarian formula is incapable of strict or formal proof, there is, he informs us, "a larger meaning of the word 'proof' " according to which a question may still be decided by the faculty of reason and not merely by resort to intuition: "Considerations may be presented capable of determining the intellect either to give or withhold its assent to the doctrine and this is equivalent to proof." [17] The question now is, what are the "philosophical grounds" which might lead us to accept the first principle of a moral doctrine? Mill's reply is to produce his notorious analogy between "visible" and "see" on the one hand and "desirable" and "desire" on the other.[18]

What is the force of this argument? The answer to this question is much contested. Within the last few years there has been a spate of articles on Mill's 'proof' of utility. Nor is this very surprising for he is raising for consideration and dealing in a highly thoughtful manner with what is the most fundamental yet perplexing issue of ethical theory. As a result of the recent discussions of Mill's argument one thing at least seems reasonably clear: He is here remaining faithful to his distinction between science and art and is *not* offering a formal proof of his fundamental principle. Even so, Mill's argument is so elusive and has given rise to such conflicting and complex interpretations that one cannot feel altogether confident even about this conclusion. While it would lead me too far afield to examine these various interpretations, I regard the issue as so important for the later stages of my argument in this chapter that I can scarcely avoid attempting a brief, if tentative assessment of what it is Mill is striving to establish in the first part of his proof of the principle of utility.

In the first place, Mill's argument from analogy may, I believe, be seen as deriving from his fundamental empiricist assumptions. He may be understood as laying down a quite general meta-moral principle, namely that nothing can rationally be credited with being an ultimate moral end unless a ground for doing so can be found in some *experience.* Just as we could not hope to convince people that something is visible unless they can actually see it, so, in the case of morality, we cannot hope to convince people that something is good unless they already tend to desire it or could

---
[17] U, p.4.
[18] *Ibid.,* p.32.

be brought to desire it. When Mill claims that "If the end which the utilitarian doctrine proposes to itself were not, in theory and practice, acknowledged to be an end, nothing could ever convince any person that it was so",[19] then he may be understood as issuing a reminder. He reminds us that it is at least a necessary condition of its being judged worthwhile that any such end be grounded in some actual or potential human desires. Indeed, unless there were such a connection between moral principles and human nature it is hard to see how they could ever get a grip on our feelings or inclinations and so function as guides to conduct.

Thus I interpret Mill as making a minimal claim: that for an end to be good it must at least *be capable of being wanted or desired.* It might be objected that it is more plausible to interpret him in the traditional manner - as making the larger claim that being desired is a necessary and sufficient condition for being an ultimate end. To adopt this traditional interpretation, though, would be to saddle Mill with a blatant inconsistency, since he designates as morally vicious such natural or instinctive desires as selfishness, destructiveness, love of dominance, cruelty and so forth. Hence, in his view, a thing's *being desired* cannot even, in any straight forward manner, be regarded as a necessary criterion of its goodness. Men and women desire certain things which are immoral and their desires for those things ought to be repressed or at least regulated. On the other hand, there are various ideal ends which, though not originally desired except as a means to happiness come, through moral education, to be desired in and for themselves. Thus, being desired may, in a somewhat altered sense of that expression, continue to be regarded as necessarily a criterion of an ultimate end, i.e. it must be possible for men to be morally trained so that they come to find certain ideal ends intrinsically desirable.

The above reading of Mill has the advantage of being consonant with Mill's persistent view that any attempt to deduce an ultimate end directly from the facts of human nature is impossible in principle. By contrast, if his 'proof' is understood (as it often is) as an attempt to found an argument for the desirability of an ultimate end on man's supposed universal tendency to desire it, then Mill must be supposed to have fallen into a fairly blatant inconsistency. Furthermore, the interpretation I favour

---

[19] U, p.32.

remains compatible with Mill's moral individualism, in particular with the requirement that, in the final resort, a man must not be dictated to by the facts if he is to be free to make his own commitment to ultimate moral principles.

All the same, this advance does not extricate Mill from his every difficulty. The only reason so far offered for taking self-development to be the ultimate end is that some people are already known to desire it and all others (allegedly) have the potential to do so. Given the proper training and environment all will, we are urged to believe, become capable of aiming at self-development as an ideal end. Now, from the fact that some men and women come to acquire the desire for self-perfection it follows (trivially) that self-perfection is an end susceptible of engaging desire. But why, it may be asked, *ought* they desire self-development?

The Appeal to Competent Judges

How, then, is this ultimate standard of conduct to be vindicated? In Mill's terms, if the standard is to be "rational" it must be derived from experience. Not, of course, from the experience of mankind at large, but from "the feelings and judgment of the experienced" - of those, that is to say, whose distinctively human potentialities have been trained and cultivated and are already flourishing.

The point of this, the second stage of Mill's argument in defence of his ultimate principle, is to show that the life of self-perfection can be justified because anyone who has experienced both that life and a life devoted to the lower or bodily pleasures will readily admit that the intellectual, spiritual and morally responsible life is intrinsically superior. Having introduced the qualitative distinction between "higher and "lower" pleasures, Mill goes on to contend that the higher pleasures are always to be preferred. How can we establish that this is the case? Only by appealing to those who are most competent to judge, that is to say, to the wise and the cultivated. "Now it is an unquestionable fact", he claims, "that those who are equally acquainted with, and equallly capable of appreciating, both, do give a most marked preference to the manner of existence which employs their higher faculties". A "being of higher faculties" could never really wish to sink into what he regards as "a lower grade of existence": no intelligent person would ever agree to being changed into a fool nor would any "person of feeling and conscience" ever consent to live the "selfish and base" life of the unprincipled rogue even if such a transformation were to lead to the most complete satisfaction of the desires which they share with the ignoramus and the rascal.[20] Lower pleasures may sometimes please us more in the sense that they lead to greater satisfaction of desire; but even so higher pleasures are to be preferred, and the only evidence it is possible to provide for this contention - the only way in which we can refute Bentham's claim that "quantity of pleasure being equal pushpin is as good as poetry" - is to appeal to the nearly unanimous preference of competent judges.

Mill's attempt to establish that some pleasures are higher or more valuable than others has often been treated with scant respect. Maurice Cowling, though, overreaches himself more than most in attempting to rebut Mill. He objects that it is not true "that all, or most, men always, or usually, do desire the higher cultivation at the expense of 'the lower' ".[21] What Cowling here denies, Mill never asserts; indeed Mill fully admits the point on which Cowling's idle objection turns. Consider another example of the tactic of contemptuous dismissal. Shirley Letwin writes off Mill's argument as a poorly disguised attempt to foist the preferences of the superior few on the many: "Mill", she says, "carelessly knocked down the barricades piled up by Bentham against the tyranny of those who claimed to know how their neighbour should live".[22] It is not planned to settle here the question whether Mill's argument may properly be said to carry illiberal implications; this is a matter which is to be taken up in a late chapter. Surely the first thing to do is to examine his argument in order to see whether there is anything in it *as an argument.* In my view, the argument does deserve to be taken seriously, even if on closer examination it turns out to require qualification.

Why should it be thought that the verdict of the competent judge cannot be an adequate test for determining which of two pleasures is to be

---

[20] *Ibid.,* p.8.
[21] M. Cowling, *op.cit.,* p.53.
[22] Shirley Robin Letwin, *op.cit.,* p.306.

preferred on qualitative grounds? One of the stock criticisms is that Mill's argument is circular. For the competent judge must be picked out in virtue of having certain qualifications and it looks as if these qualifications must include his preferring the higher pleasures. And once this is allowed, Mill has tacitly (it is argued) admitted having prior knowledge of what is to count as higher pleasure and so has no need to invoke the competent judge. Mill, it seems, could escape from this circle only by finding some independent way of defining competency in choosing higher pleasures.

The construction of this criticism is built on an invalid model of the notion of a competent judge. If one conceives the competent judge on the model of a competent judge of, say, good strokes in tennis, then it is easy to see how the conclusion may be derived that it is a definitive property of the competent judge that, generally speaking, the strokes he calls good are in fact (i.e. in accordance with independently specifiable criteria) good ones. The criteria for being a good judge are logically dependent on the criteria for being a good stroke. But the good judge of strokes in tennis does not provide an analogue for Mill's competent judge of higher pleasures. For Mill's criterion of being a competent judge is having had the requisite wide experience of pleasures of different kinds (indepedently specifiable, e.g. pleasure in pushpin, pleasure in poetry). If there is a logical link in this nexus of concepts, then it works in the opposite direction from that falsely indicated by the judge-of-good-strokes-in-tennis model. That a pleasure is preferred by those who have the requisite experience to make a comparison implies that it is a higher pleasure, not *vice versa*. As will emerge, however, I do not want to defend this strong form of Mill's thesis. I would argue for the propriety of giving weight rather than complete credence to competent judges. However that question may be decided, it is important to make the overall structure of Mill's position clear. A better model for the competent judge of higher pleasures would be the competent judge of toughness of mountains. Who can tell us whether Mount Everest is tougher to climb than Mont Blanc? We would look to the man who has tried both.

Thus the competent judge of which pleasures are higher is the man who is well acquainted with the various activities we wish to compare. I underline "activities" in order to forestall a further objection to Mill's argument before I go on to offer an extended (though partial) defence of his position. The objection to be considered now is that Mill's view assumes the possibility of intersubjective comparisons of higher and lower pleasures. For Mill's argument depends on the possiblity of a man of virtue and wisdom (someone like Mill himself) being able to reject the pleasures of the fool after comparing them with his own and finding them wanting. But "how could a Mill know", A.C. MacIntyre asks, "what it was like to be a satisfied fool, any more than the fool could know what it was like to be a Mill?"[23] What I take to be the essence of the objection MacIntyre is suggesting may be captured by observing that it would seem to be impossible for Mill to take on the fool's limitations. If *per impossibile* he did, he would, like the fool, be in a position whence it is impossible to compare the joys of poetry with the joys of pushpin. Now since he cannot and does not take on the fool's limitations, he still cannot make the relevant comparison. For what he is required to compare is not how poetry feels to a Mill with how pushpin feels to a Mill, but how poetry feels to a Mill with how pushpin feels to a fool.

If Mill's argument is interpreted as requiring the competent judge to make the comparison between higher and lower *pleasures* then one can agree with MacIntyre that it can hardly be sustained. But, as I have already stated,[24] it is quite consistent with my interpretation of Mill to understand his qualitative distinction between pleasures as a distinction not between pleasures but between *activities*. If the distinction is so interpreted, the argument from the competent judges may, I believe, be seen as at least a plausible justification of self-perfection as the supreme value of morals and politics. While Mill does want to give a justification of the cultivation of the higher powers in terms of a superior pleasure, from the point of view of justifying his liberalism this is something of a red herring. For this purpose, it will be all the same if we ignore the consideration of superior and inferior pleasures and interpret Mill as attempting simply to assert the intrinsic superiority of certain activities, rather than the pleasures associated with them.

Once this is said, however, it becomes evident that the poetry/pushpin argument needs a certain amount of refinement if it is to be

---

[23] A.C. MacIntyre, *A Short History of Ethics* (New York, 1966), p.236. Cf. Maurice Cowling, *op.cit.,* pp.53-54.
[24] In Chapter III.

of use to Mill. In particular, the status of the pushpin-player needs further specifying. A person of such low native endowment that playing pushpin is for him a feat of intellectual and practical skill may, presumably, experience in pushpin the nearest thing for him possible to the pleasures extolled by Mill and to be derived from the exercise and development of one's active powers. By the same token, he is, presumably, not an appropriate choice for Mill's pushpin-player. An appropriate choice must be a man capable of or able to become capable of more demanding feats, yet restricted by circumstance to looking no higher than pushpin. It is still the case that a Mill cannot entirely enter into his situation. It is by no means so clear, though, that a Mill cannot make the relevant comparison. The man of high sophistication can recall stages in his development when his sophistication was less. He can remember entering with zest into situations then fresh and challenging, now trite and boring to him. And he can sensibly ask and answer the question which condition he prefers. He can do this as long as he remembers the choice is not between the old activity and the new, given the new sophistication both times, but between the old activity undertaken with the old crude approach and the new activity handled with the new sophisitcation. If we ask him which situation he would rather be in, then, he can make a sensible reply. What the reply will be is not completely obvious, though I am quite prepared to concede that the odds favour a preference for the new sophistication.

If we ask another question, though, namely the question which of the two situations does he *choose* to be in, then it does become obvious he *cannot* answer that he chooses the old naivety. There is this time little point in his answering either way, since one cannot choose to resume naivety. One might perhaps plan to some extent to put oneself in the way of an increase in naivety, say by the use of drugs as well as by less drastic and less effective methods. Still, the acquisition of sophistication is not in any obvious way a reversible process. One might and, as one grows older, customarily does suffer some decline of powers, but not normally by working towards this end.

Thus we may agree for our purposes to take Mill's argument in the following way. The wise and virtuous man comes to prefer poetry to pushpin because certain of its characteristic features make it highly conducive to his self-development. Some activities are preferable to others because they are bound up with the development of our higher powers. Reading the poetry of Wordsworth, for example, is a way of perfecting our aesthetic susceptibilities, whereas pushpin scarcely begins to call any of our higher faculties into play. Devotion to science and history and an active participation in social and political affairs is going to test and strengthen our nobler capacities while addiction to mere money-grubbing or to the self-indulgence typical of the aristocracy will only weaken and damage the intellectual and moral powers. Furthermore, it matters a great deal to the cultivated that they should live in one way rather than another. The person with a cultivated mind acquires a sense of dignity roughly equivalent to his degree of mental cultivation; because of this he can never really wish to sink into a way of life he thinks of as inferior or continue to pursue what he regards as evil or relatively worthless activities.

Interpreted in the above way, Mill's argument does not require that the experienced or cultivated person be capable of comparing his own *pleasures* with those of the uncultivated. All it requires is that he be able to compare both sets of *activities* and observe that his own possess certain characteristics which the other lacks. Having made that comparison, the cultivated man (Mill may be understood as claiming) feels somehow impelled to opt for the superior activity rather than the inferior. At this point in his reasoning Mill is tacitly invoking the Socratic doctrine that virtue is knowledge. Mill is not saying that because the educated man finds poetry, say, to be an important element in his life he is therefore entitled to *deduce* from this fact the conclusion that poetry is preferable to pushpin. No, the connection Mill is alluding to is not logical but *psychological:* once an educated man really comes to appreciate the nature of an aesthetic activity like the reading of poetry or an intellectual one like the study of history he will never, *as a matter of fact,* voluntarily forego them for a life given over to crime or to the gratification of a succession of bodily appetites. Over-indulgence in inferior, sensuous modes of living or the pursuit of a life of vice derives from *ignorance,* from the fact that those who engage in such activities "know only their own side of the question". Whilst the educated man knows, from personal observation and study, the characteristics and consequences of such activities, and so feels no inclination to pursue them.

To the objection that one can point to examples of back-sliding which serve to undermine his hypothesis, Mill has a persuasive if not wholly convincing retort. The objector might well argue, in the words Mill puts into his mouth, that there are some men who "pursue sensual indulgences to the injury of health, though perfectly aware that health is the greater good" and others who, while beginning with "youthful enthusiasn for everything noble, as they advance in years sink into indolence and selfishness.".25 Still, if we looked more closely at cases like these we would always find that the people concerned did not "voluntarily choose" the lower mode of existence in favour of the higher. There are two possibilities. Either they opt for the lower mode because they no longer have physical access to the higher, or, having gradually ceased to be capable of enjoying the good life, they are not longer able to appreciate its character and so are incapable of making a genuine choice.

In thus attempting to justify certain activities as being more worthwhile than others Mill should not be understood as intimating there is only one path to self-development. On his view there are a number of different roads to self-perfection, a number of equally legitimate ways of developing our distinctive human powers. Whilst it would certainly be wrong to starve any of the higher capacities, any man with, say, some understanding of science or history might still find himself drawn away from a professional or academic life towards one in which he was most concerned with the intense cultivation of a few personal relationships or in which his energies were channelled into some artistic endeavour or into social or political participation. Such a man would, though, always be attracted by acticivies of comparable quality; activities which would in some way be conducive to the growth of his human potentialities. After trying out and appreciating a life exercising his higher faculties it would be impossible for him to choose to sink back into a style of living which provided them with little or no sustenance.

In conclusion, we may credit Mill with having made out a plausible case for taking the ideal of self-perfection, as the highest good and as the basis of his liberalism. By appealing to what educated and intelligent persons value most when they are in a position to compare the character of various human activities he provides a ground for saying that what is taken to be most valuable under such circumstances is indeed worth pursuing for

---

25 U, p.9.

its own sake. It does not follow logically that what educated and intelligent persons most prefer is valuable because they prefer it, but their preferring it (under the conditions Mill specifies) is a *good reason* for claiming it to be of supreme value.

The interpretation I have given of Mill's argument from the competent judge thus attributes to him not the claim that the judge is infallible, but a weaker claim which I believe to be defensible as the stronger claim is not. In my view, it is reasonable to weigh more carefully what, for instance, a great writer, or a gifted teacher says about the value of his own undertakings than what is said about them by people we know not to have had comparable experience of the activities in question and so to be not in a position to understand the point of those activities. It may without damage to this contention be granted that if we are to avoid the naturalistic fallacy we cannot immediately conclude the judgment of our authority is sufficient to establish that the activity in question is worthwhile. All my interpretation does is to point to the judge or expert as a useful guide in the selection of worthwhile activities. For this reason the expert is not (contrary to Letwin's allegation) to be understood as a moral dictator. My interpretation envisages a situation which seems not unrealistic or unreasonable, viz. that certain persons, because of their having compared certain activities, may come to be good judges of their relative value; and, further, that their ability to judge is something which can be both recognised and esteemed by others.

Mill's justification of the good life is defensible, but it is certainly not incontrovertible, as Mill himself would doubtless have been the first to admit. Further, full-scale defence of the Socratic doctrine that virtue is knowledge (on which Mill relies) would be well beyond the scope of my thesis, where my primary purpose is to consider the problem it raises for the justification of Mill's liberalism. It would certainly be part of my task, though, to point to any major inconsistency in Mill's doctrine. Discussion is therefore owing of whether it is possible to accommodate into Mill's doctrine without inconsistency the strand of thought I have shown to rely on the Socratic notion of the natual goodness of man. In particular, as I have intimated already, it might well be felt that this strand is irreconcilable with Mill's central doctrine of moral individualism, which requires the autonomy of morals.

Self-Development and
The Autonomy of Morals

If the highest end of moral activity were simply laid down for us by the preference of competent judges, there would be, it appears, no place left for moral individualism. Moral individualism requires that we be left free to decide what is the supreme goal of morals and politics. Yet if the supreme goal is derived from the fact that once having really appreciated the character of the higher activities a man will always opt for them, then we do seem obliged to accept as of the highest moral worth a predetermined goal, unalterable by human decision. While human nature remains unchanged in the relevant respect, there would on this view be only *one correct* answer to the question what is the supreme end of morals and politics. Yet the moral individualist demand for the final right of the individual to decide for himself the ultimate end of the good life is put forward as more than a mere demand that people should be licensed to make errors on this subject, though licence to make errors is part of what is demanded. The thorough-going moral individualist is committed to the claim that our ultimate moral and political valuations should be determined by no standards except those we choose for ourselves. This means that at the very least there has to be a diversity of *valid,* final moral and political ends, any of which a man might properly decide to put first.

The apparent contradiction here can be eased, though not, I think, wholly dissolved. On the one hand, one might draw attention to the, in one sense, 'contentless' nature of the Millian supreme moral and political goal. As I have said earlier, because of the diverse characters of individual men, the goal of self-development may be realised in diverse ways. A man might be pursuing his self-development *in primarily pursuing* some specific activity such as solving problems in mathematics or securing some political objective, in the pursuit of which he develops his particular powers or potentialities. He does not develop his abstract, contentless self, but he develops the individual character that he has. So that while he properly chooses from among a diversity of specific activities which he might validly take as a primary goal, he is in so doing, as a matter of objective fact though not necessarily as a matter of subjective intention, pursuing the general human goal of self-development. By thus distinguishing between subjective and objective pursuits one might seem to effect a reconciliation between the doctrine of self-development and the extreme moral individualist emphasis on the *choice* of final goals.

On the other hand, Mill does set some limits to the area of valid moral choice available to men. Whilst he certainly wants men left free to make invalid moral choices if they must, he does not want to eliminate the idea of an invalid choice. He does want to say that some *wrong* choices are made, that there are some roads which lead not to self-development but to self-frustration or even to self-destruction. Nor, as I have pointed out in some detail, is the development of just any potentiality to count as self-development in his sense. Mill has a fairly comprehensive but at the same time definite and bounded conception of the good man. For him it is only the development of the higher human capabilities that is to count as self-development. And the general area available to make valid choices in, the area we are to take as that of the higher human capabilities, is determined by the experience of the competent judges. It is in this way that the Greek doctrine of self-development does circumscribe Mill's moral individualism. Between the Greek doctrine and what may be called an absolute moral individualism there is, then, a residual contradiction. The absolute moral individualist claims for men final authority to choose their own concept of the 'good man'; he claims any such choice whatever is a valid choice. Mill may be said to adhere not to such an absolute moral individualism, but to a moral individualism tempered by his giving some content and thus setting some bounds to the kind of life it is good for a man to choose.

Where we are given a picture, however broad, of the good life for man, there is always the possibility of dispute about this picture. From the spirit of Mill's liberalism, he could reasonably be interpreted as welcoming such dispute. While he remained Aristotelian in believing it possible to be right or wrong about the essentials of the kind of life it is good for a man to live, it would be in line with his fallibilist approach for him to put forward his own broad picture of the good life as provisional and disputable at its boundaries. In the advanced societies of today we live in a world of a number of different, overlapping and competing moralities, each appealing to its own concept of man and each providing a somewhat different account of man's essential 'needs' or potentialities. Because of his opposition to moral dogmatism and his insistence that diversity of views and of lives is conducive to discovery in morality as well as in other areas, we may take it that Mill would have welcomed the exploration of moral problems arising out of the co-operation and conflict of diverse moralities. We may also take it that he meant to leave room within his own doctrine for the possibility of change and revision.

PART II

THE SCOPE AND LIMITS OF LIBERTY

CHAPTER VIII

SELF-DEVELOPMENT, PROGRESS AND THE FREEDOM OF THE MAJORITY

Self-Development and Progress

John Stuart Mill inherited, and never abandoned, the eighteenth century faith in perfectibility. The basis of Mill's inherited faith in human progress was his associationist psychology, to which he adhered throughout his life. Associationism taught him to deny all innate or 'natural' differences of capacity between men and so held out the possibility of human progress. Of his father's theories, "none was more important", Mill wrote, than his "fundamental doctrine" of "the formation of all human character by circumstances, through the universal Principle of Association, and the consequent unlimited possiblity of improving the moral and intellectual condition of mankind by education."[1] Men's characters are thus the outcome of their circumstances and since their circumstances can be changed their characters are susceptible of indefinite improvement. For James Mill the belief in progress is supported by an appeal to science, to the new scientific psychology of associationism. Education becomes an all-important instrument available to the present generation which enables it to produce a new generation of men who will be superior to their fathers. This educability, this perfectibility, is what distinguishes mankind from the rest of

---
[1] *Autobiography, op.cit.,* p.75.

the animal realm. "That he is a *progressive* being, is the great distinction of man; he is the only progressive being on the globe."[2]

It would seem that one thing James Mill is pointing to when he describes man as a "progressive being" is a fundamental fact about human nature, a fact upon which any belief in progress must be seen to depend. To hold a belief in progress is at least to believe men and women capable of learning from experience and of adapting themselves and their situation in the light of knowledge gained from experience. They must be supposed capable of modifying their environment in accordance with their desires, of planning for the future, and of foregoing present pleasures for the sake of future ones. So much, if not more, is involved in the Benthamite conception of progress.

John Stuart Mill inherited his father's belief in the educability of man. Indeed, he thought of himself as a living exemplification of the soundness of his father's belief in the importance of an early and sound intellectual training.[3] But education is, for J.S. Mill, not merely a matter of intellectual training in the sense of the cultivation of a spirit of critical inquiry and the acquisition of a body of knowledge. Education is primarily the cultivation of individual character. This includes not only the development of a critical and inquiring mind but also the growth of our moral, aesthetic and emotional capacities. Moral and aesthetic education is of particular importance, involving as it does the cultivation of our feelings, and so encouraging us to sympathise with others, control our selfish desires and associate our own self-development and happiness with the self-development and happiness of others.

Education and Goodness

By education, then, Mill has in mind the cultivation and development (by a wide variety of means) of our distinctively human capacities. For Mill, a man's individual character is created only by "civilization, instruction,

---

[2] James Mill, *Education,* Supplement to the Sixth Edition of The Encyclopaedia Brittanica, 1824, p.14.
[3] *Autobiography, op.cit.,* p.21.

education, culture,"4 that is to say, man develops his characteristically human excellence primarily by artificial means. Accordingly, it is no more than a sentimental error to speak, as did Rousseau, of the natural goodness of man. "It is only", Mill writes, "in a highly artificialized condition of human nature that the notion grew up or, I believe, ever could have grown up that goodness was natural, because only after a long course of artificial education did good sentiments become so habitual, and so predominant over bad, as to arise unprompted when occasion called for them."5 Human virtues, Mill is saying, are not natural, they are preeminently the results of education: even justice is, according to him an artificial virtue. Civilization, in Mill's view, is man's continuous and never ending effort to tame and subordinate the merely animal or organic desires and impulses so that "the qualities which are the distinctive endowment of a human being" may be enabled to take root, come to maturity and be allowed to flourish.

Mill, it has been claimed, goes too far in his insistence on the need to repress the gratification of our natural instincts. He is alleged to have urged "an all-out war against instinct" and the degree of his success in this campaign is supposed to be measured by the extraordinary latter-day popularity of psychoanalysis.6 But this charge, it seems fair to say, amounts to little more than a piece of gratuitous extravagance on the part of its author. The truth is Mill wishes to starve only the "bad instincts" and willingly agrees that most of our "natural impulses", or instincts, "ought to be only regulated, not repressed."7 Among the instincts which he *would* wish suppressed he specifically mentions such thoroughly undesirable propensities as destructiveness - the desire to destroy for the sake of destroying; domination, or the sheer delight in exercising inordinate power over others; and natural or "voluptuous" cruelty.8 What is more, the emphasis here on the need to regulate but not extirpate the majority of our natural impulses is quite characteristic of Mill's view of this question. Consider, for instance, his objection to the Calvinist theory which would

---

4 OL, p.115.
5 "Nature" in G. Nakhnikian (ed.), *John Stuart Mill, Nature and Utility of Religion* (New York, 1958) p.32. Quoted by J.B. Schneewind, *Mill's Ethical Writings, op.cit.,* p.26.
6 Sheldon S. Wolin, *Politics and Vision* (London, 1960) p.318.
7 "'Nature", *op.cit.,* pp.38-39.
8 *Ibid.,* p.39.

insist on our strongest inclinations being "rooted out and consumed". In opposition to this doctrine he commends "' Pagan self-assertion' " as a necessary part of the good life. "Those who have most natural feeling are always those whose cultivated feelings may be made the strongest;" and the truth is that "desires and impulses are as much a part of a perfect human being as beliefs and restraints: and strong impulses are only perilous when not properly balanced."[9]

The whole point of self-development, Mill is arguing, is not to follow our original nature, but to cultivate and improve it: "There is hardly anything valuable in the natural man except capacities - a whole world of possibilities, all of them dependent upon eminently artificial discipline for being realized."[10] His view is in other words, that the only thing valuable which is natural to man is a range of potentialities - potentialities for acquiring the various higher abilities which distinguish civilized life from the life of man in his natural or savage state. If, then, we should wish to adopt the conception of conforming to nature as a model for an ethical code then "the only nature which it is ever commendable to follow" is the "artificially created or at least artificially perfected nature of the best and noblest human beings."[11]

Mill's doctrine of self-development is a doctrine of progress both individual and social. Man is "a progressive being": the conception of individual (and social) progress is woven into the very fabric of Mill's liberalism. The individual (and society) progresses or develops by becoming more civilized or cultivated, by rising above the level of the 'natural' state, whether individual or social. Mill (in various places in his writings) distinguishes between a narrower and a broader sense of progress or civilization. In the narrower sense progress is identical with the advance of commercial and industrial civilization, viz. with the "progress of national prosperity, of industry and wealth". In the broader sense "progress" (or "civilization") is equivalent to "human improvement", to being "further advanced in the road to perfection; happier, nobler, wiser".[12] When Mill uses the terms "progress" or "social progress" he normally has in

---

[9] OL, pp.118-120.
[10] "Nature", *op.cit.,* p.32.
[11] *Ibid.,* p.37.
[12] "Civilization" in G. Himmelfarb *op.cit.,* pp.45-46.

mind this broader sense, what we should now customarily refer to as moral progress. Progress in this second sense, then, consists in the improvement of man himself, in the individual progress or development of human beings. In the *Liberty* Mill takes his ultimate stand on this kind of progress, on what he calls "utility in the largest sense, grounded on the permanent interests of man as a progressive being." The most vital of these interests is "individual spontaneity" or "individuality" since where it is lacking "there is wanting one of the principal ingredients of human happiness, and quite the chief ingredient of individual and social progress."[13] He believed, with Comte, that the "natural progress of society consists in the growth of our human attributes, comparatively to our animal and our purely organic ones. . ."[14] In Mill's view progress consists principally in the improvement of man himself, in the development of his "Moral, intellectual, and aesthetic faculties."[15]

He did not regard progress as inevitable; it was uncertain and depended upon conditions which might not always be present. All men and women, Mill believed, have the "need" or potentiality for self-development. Given a whole range of pre-conditions and opportunities (non-interference, social diversity, social and moral consensus, democratic participation, the expansion of formal education, the reduction of poverty and disease, greater economic and social equality, etc.) each person will be able to call upon his own "inward forces" and in thus exercising his individuality will be so much nearer self-perfection. There is nothing in the nature of human beings themselves which would prevent their attaining the dignity of thinking and feeling beings. But owing chiefly to their wretched social conditions "even the men and women who inhabit the more civilized parts of the world," though not altogether undeveloped, "are but starved specimens of what nature can and will produce."[16] Any person whose human potentialities have begun to emerge, who has been taught in some degree to exercise his faculties and to whom the "fountains of knowledge" have been opened "finds sources of inexhaustible interest" in all that

---

[13] OL, p.74.
[14] J.S. Mill, *Auguste Comte and Positivism* (University of Michigan, 1961) p.100. And see also Errol Harris, "John Stuart Mill's Theory of Progress," *Ethics,* Vol.LXVI, No.3.
[15] *Auguste Comte and Positivism, op.cit.,* p.100.
[16] OL, p.117. U, pp.9-10.

surrounds him, "in the objects of nature, the achievements of art, the imaginations of poetry, the incidents of history, the ways of mankind, past and present, and their prospects in the future." All young people may be said to have the need or potentiality for the growth of their nobler feelings and powers, but in most the seed never germinates owing to lack of education and to an unfavourable social environment. Unless the environment is propitious their finer feelings and higher capacities wither before they have a chance to develop, with the result that most people never achieve their proper end. Mill writes:

> "Capacity for the nobler feelings is in most natures a very tender plant, easily killed, not only by hostile influences, but by mere want of sustenance; and in the majority of young persons it speedily dies away if the occupations to which their position in life has devoted them and the society into which it has thrown them are not favourable to keeping that higher capacity in exercise."[17]

The reason why most men and women care little for the life of self-perfection is that they have never really *experienced* it; never having had the opportunity to give the free and the good life a fair trial they are unable to appreciate its intrinsic superiority. At the present comparatively unadvanced stage of civilisation it is only the educated and cultivated few who have been initiated into those intellectual, artistic, scientific and practical activities which do most to promote their individuality and develop their higher natures. Only when the "present wretched education, and wretched social arrangements" are amended will the personalities of the mass of the people begin to unfold as they should. Yet even now a considerable minority do manage to develop their higher powers and acquire a sense of dignity; and this is "so essential a part of the happiness of those in whom it is strong, that nothing which conflicts with it could be otherwise than momentarily an object of desire to them."[18]

Mill, as I have said and as is clear from the foregoing account, did not believe progress inevitable. Individual and social progress depended chiefly upon "education," in the widest sense of that word. By "education" Mill meant all the cultural circumstances which operate as factors in the formation of individual character and he especially emphasised the

---

[17] U, pp.9-10.
[18] U, p.9.

correlation between individual character and specific social and politicial institutions. Individual (and social) progress depended mainly upon creating the type of liberal society which would stimulate and promote self-activity. Largely because of his great confidence in the power of ideas to change men's characters and to alter social arrangements, Mill continued to believe in the possiblity of moving slowly towards such a society. Although, as I have indicated, he did not hold progress to be inevitable in principle, he did believe that as a matter of fact, except for "occasional and temporary exceptions", there was a general tendency to progress - "a tendency towards a better and happier state."[19]

Progress and the Freedom of the Majority

My account of Mill's theory of individual and social progress has focussed on its reliance on a conception of the individual as capable of perfecting himself by exercising independent judgment and rational choice. To this it might be objected that while such might be a correct account of Mill's conception of the *ideal* individual - of man at his best - Mill was very far from supposing that all men and women do or ever could possess the capacity for rational self-determination. Here is raised the serious problem of Mill's view of the capacities and potentialities of the majority, and if the foregoing objection could be pressed home it would undermine my own interpretation of Mill's theory of individual and social progress.

On a first and perhaps even subsequent reading of Mill it would seem that this may be one of the issues about which he could never make up his mind but wavered between one position and another, here between undue pessimism and uncalled for optimism. This possiblity raises a serious problem, one concerning not only Mill's outlook on the future progress of mankind but also his views on the defence of liberty and on the characteristics of liberal-democracy. Its bearing on the questions of liberty and of democracy will be touched upon later. For the moment I shall content myself with defending my account of Mill's theory of progress. If, however, my defence can be sustained it will be seen to have important implications for the other questions as well.

---

[19] *Logic, op.cit.,* p.596.

Now, it is certainly not too difficult for anyone to show that Mill held a fairly low opinion of the capacity of the majority for independent thought and rational discussion. As I have already argued in my ChapterV, Mill elaborates the concept of individuality by contrasting the individualist, the critical, morally responsible person, with the 'mass man', the conformist who relies on no faculty except the "ape-like one of imitation." Mill was far from overestimating the maturity or rationality of the majority of men and women of his own day. It is the merest caricature of his views to suggest (as some have done) that he thought of ordinary human beings as growing up in the image of himself. Anyone who can speak of "the stupidity and habitual indifference of the mass of mankind,"[20] of the "present low state of the human mind,"[21] or who can conclude that "society has now fairly got the better of individuality" can hardly be accused of exaggerating the mental and moral powers of the average man. In what reads like a considered judgment, Mill sums up the majority of his contemporaries as "not only moderate in intellect, but also moderate in inclinations."[22] And this assessment, it might be added, does seem pretty realistic, especially when it is recalled Mill was writing before the advent of universal, compulsory education and the full emergence of democracy.

Taking his departure from an examination of *On Liberty* in which he highlights Mill's view of the majority as lacking in self-determination, Richard B. Friedman has recently been led to a radical reassessment of Mill's theory of progress.[23] His thesis is that "Mill is prepared to argue that 'progress' has not and, moreover, can not succeed in transforming every human being into that independent, rational individual, capable of and willing to make up his mind, who is at once the ideal and the presupposition of liberalism" (p.292). Mill came to see that only a small minority of men in modern, democratic societies exhibit any degree of autonomy; the majority have no desire to be self-determining and display an eager wilingness to submit to authority. What is more, his theory of history led Mill to regard this state of affairs as characteristic of a "natural" state of society. Mill saw

---
[20] *Letters,* (Elliott ed.) Vol.1, pp.162-63. Quoted by S.R. Letwin, *op.cit.,* p.295.
[21] OL, p.124; cf. *Autobiography, op.cit.,* p.162.
[22] OL, p.126.
[23] Richard B. Friedman, *op.cit., passim.*

himself as living through an age of transition which was rapidly coming to an end and ushering in a new organic period, a mass society in which the majority would "revert to their natural state of willing dependence on authority." (p.293) In these circumstances, one of Mill's basic problems in *On Liberty* was that of providing a justification of liberty for those who do not desire liberty. Accordingly, in Chapter III he is said to be found arguing that self-determination or individuality may be vindicated as possessing intrinsic value only for an intellectual and moral elite; for the majority it can be given only an instrumental justification - by persuading them that the right and capacity for individuality of the elite is a *sine qua non* of social, i.e. material progress.

Friedman's interpretation has the merit of seeming to suggest a way in which Mill's passionate concern for individuality might be reconciled with his belief in the importance of a clerisy. The argument might run: because the majority is neither desirous nor capable of self-determination there exists a need and justification for a clerisy. But would not such a reconciliation be at the expense of Mill's liberalism? Friedman thinks not: he tries to forestall the objection that he is forcing Mill's thought into an authoritarian mould. Since the freedom of the elite is the mainspring of material progress, it is in the best interests of the majority to be guided by the elite. This does not mean, however, that the elite is entitled to coerce the many for their own good. Its use of coercion would not only be corrupting to the elite, but would thwart the desires of the majority and make them unfree. For while the majority "buckle under the responsibility of having to make their 'own' choices" (p.289) and happily defer to custom and authority, this does not mean that they "desire to be coerced, that is, desire to be restrained from doing what they desire." (p.290) Friedman's point is that since "the absence of external coercion" is the meaning liberty usually has for Mill and since he always regards this liberty as of great intrinsic value to the majority, Mill remains firmly within the liberal tradition.

But Friedman's disavowal will not do, for while it rules out Mill's condonation of the direct coercion of the majority it leaves him saddled with a disguised paternalism. The majority are said to be free insofar as they do what they desire, and one of their predominant desires is to submit to the authoirty of an elite. Thus is the elite were to indoctrinate them so as to strengthen their desire for submission, if would follow that their freedom would *ipso facto* be increased. Yet surely they would then no longer be called free by anyone, least of all by Mill. So Friedman's reinterpretation of Mill yields a very unpalatable conclusion.

Of course it may be that Mill himself *was* incoherent, that he overlooked the paternalistic implications of his pessimism concerning the self-determining capacity of the majority. That such is not the case, however, begins to be seen if we examine Friedman's account of Mill's "answer" to the charge of paternalism. As Friedman presents it, part of Mill's answer is: "the majority are entitled to free development (even though they are indifferent to it.)" (p.302). But it is an absurdity to say that the majority are "entitled" to something they are intrinsically incapable of desiring. Friedman is driven to father this absurdity on Mill, because his own thesis will not allow him to accept Mill's argument at its face value. Mill's contested argument (previously quoted by Friedman (p.301)), is that paternalistic rule by an elite is "inconsistent with the freedom and development of all the rest . . ." As this passage suggests, Mill is resolutely opposed to paternalism not so much because he values non-interference in and for itself as because paternalism denies the status of men and women as independent agents: by frustrating their desires, compulsion inhibits choice and so stifles self-development. Mill explains:

> "To be prevented from doing what one is inclined to, or from acting according to one's own judgement of what is desirable, is not only always irksome, but always tends, *pro tanto,* to stunt the development of some portion of the bodily or mental faculties, either sensitive or active . . ."[24]

At the very foundation of Mill's liberalism is his belief in self-development, or self-perfection, as the highest object men and women can pursue; and, as we have already noted, self-determination, or individuality, is both the principal condition of and the chief ingredient in the developed or perfected self. Furthermore, as we have also observed, for Mill, man is "a progressive being;" the conception of individual (and social) progress is built into his liberalism. He believed that after the basic wants for food and warmth have been satisfied, liberty or "spontaneity" is the strongest desire of human nature. Moreover, once people have some measure of autonomy, or moral freedom, they acquire a continuous desire to enlarge it; the desire for

---

[24] *Principles of Political Economy:* London: Longmans, 1866: Book V, Ch.XI, Sec.2, p.569. All succeeding references to the *Principles* will be to this edition, which will be represented by the abbreviation PPE.

independence "increases instead of diminishing in intensity as the intelligence and moral faculties are more developed."[25]

Yet while he always retained a strong belief in the possibility of human progress Mill did not delude himself into thinking the majority of his contemporaries had travelled very far along the road to perfection. Friedman misses Mill's ubiquitous assumption of the distinction between men and women as they are at the present stage of historical development and as they are potentially, that is, as they are capable of becoming. Mill thought of himself as living in a "comparatively early stage of human advancement". Though the men and women of civilized nations are so far developed as to have "attained the capacity of being guided to their own improvement by conviction or persuasion,"[26] they are still "but starved specimens of what nature can and will produce."[27] Now it may indeed be freely conceded to Friedman that modern societies, in Mill's view, do contain a preponderance of men and women who "refuse to make their own choices" (Friedman, p.189) and that individuality is grossly undervalued. But then Mill attributes this state of affairs to a combination of wretched natural and social conditions, bad laws, and the rise of social forces and intellectual movements favourable to social conformity. *Pace* Friedman, Mill sees nothing in the nature of human beings themselves which would prevent their attaining the dignity of self-determining beings. Given a whole array of pre-conditions - the reduction of poverty and disease, the expansion of formal education, a wide range of specific liberties, social diversity, moral consensus, democratic participation, greater economic and social equaity - all citizens will gradually come to acquire a greater measure of self-determination and self-development.

Because of his deep antipathy to paternalism Mill utterly rejects all theories which claim the majority should be submissively dependent on authority. Thus he rejects political despotism (except for backward nations) principally on the ground of its incompatibility with the intitiative and self-development of the citizens.[28] His chief argument for democracy is that

---

[25] PPE Book II, Ch.1, Sec.3, p.129. Se also *The Subjection of Women* (Everyman edition, 1929) pp.312-14.
[26] OL, p.73.
[27] RG, Ch.III, pp.203-207.
[28] RG, Ch.III, pp.203-207.

since it is essential the "active faculties" should "be cultiviated not merely in a select few, but in all" it becomes of "supreme importance that all classes of the community, down to the lowest, should have much to do for themselves"[29] Again, he rejects the "dependence and protection" conception of society according to which the poor "should not be required or encouraged to think for themselves" and rejoices in the fact that the working classes are releasing themselves from the "leading strings" of their employers.[30] He is in favour of co-operative societies mainly because through them we "see our way to a change in society, which would combine the freedom and independence of the individual with the moral, intellectual and economical advantages of aggregate production."[31] Should any further evidence be required to establish Mill's antipathy to the conception of a paternalistic elite, it is to be found in a letter he wrote to Alexander Bain. From his reading of *On Liberty* Bain had taken away the impression that Mill might have meant liberal reformers ought not to endeavour to improve the intellectual powers of the majority. Mill's reply was direct and unambiguous: "the notion of an intellectual aristocracy of lumieres, while the rest of the world remains in darkness fulfills none of my aspirations - and the effort I aim at by the book is, on the contrary, to make the many more accessible to all truth by making them more open-minded."[32]

Friedman Conflates Two Distinct Theses

In what has just been said I have made it clear that Mill believes strongly in the potentiality of the majority to develop the capacity for self-determination. If Friedman is correct in attributing to Mill a directly opposed view, then Mill holds incompatible beliefs. But the truth is that Mill's position is not incoherent; rather, there is a flaw in Friedman's account of Mill. So much has already been hinted; it is now time to suggest why and where Friedman's argument goes astray. The kernel of his error is that Friedman conflates two distinct theses concerning the freedom of the majority: (1)

---

[29] PPE, Book V, Ch.XI, Sec.6, pp.572-73. Cf. OL, pp.164-65.
[30] PPE, Book IV, Ch.VII, Sec.1, pp.455-59.
[31] *Ibid.,* Book IV, Ch.VII, Sec. 7, p.476.
[32] H.S.R. Elliott (ed.) *Letters of John Stuart Mill,* 2 vols. (London, 1910) vol. I, p.223, quoted by Edward Alexander in *John Stuart Mill: Literary Essays* (New York, 1967) "Introduction" p.xx.

The majority in a modern industrial democracy conform uncritically to custom and conventional morality; thus they lack self-determination; (2) the majority in an ideal organic society would show reasoned and critical deference to those whose special enlightenment makes them an elite; in so doing they would not renounce their self-determination. Mill held both these two disctinct theses. Further, he certainly took them to be compatible and in this (a matter distinct, of course, from their truth) it is immediately evident Mill is quite correct.

In the earlier part of his article (pp.281-91) Friedman confines his attention to *On Liberty* and what I have called thesis (1). His argument is that, influenced by Tocqueville's analysis of democracy, Mill came to interpret the phrase "social tyranny" and its "reverse", "liberty" in a radical new way. "Central to this other view of 'social tyranny' is not the external coercion of the individual by society. . . . but rather the renunciation of liberty by some members of society. . . . together with the abdication of personal choice and judgment to the collectivity." (p.288)   Friedman here shows himself to be aware that Mill thinks of the majority's lack of individuality as a negative characteristic of human character correlated with the social structure of an historically novel type of society, viz. modern democratic society. As Friedman puts it, "social tyranny" is "a definitive characteristic of a particular sort of society, namely the dissolution of individuality in what has come to be called 'mass society'... it is a chief structural feature of a particular type of society." (p.295)   In other words, Friedman sees that lack of individuality is an "attribute of character" of the majority in "a particular condition of society". (p.289)   Here Friedman is right and this explains why Mill speaks of such a condition of society as a social " 'tyranny' " and as "'the only despotism of which, in the modern world, there is real danger.' " (p.291)   Mill, one can see, would scarcely have had recourse to such pejorative language had he been describing an ideal or best possible condition of society.

But Friedman then proceeds to confound this account of the condition of the majority in a mass society with Mill's account of their condition in an ideal organic society. He is led into this error through misunderstanding the nature of the deference accorded the elite by the majority in a "natural" or ideal organic society. He mistakenly equates this (reasoned and critical) deference to an elite with the conformity of the majority to "'collective authority'" in a mass society and this leads him to conclude that Mill thinks of the majority's lack of individuality as their natural or proper condition.

Friedman runs together theses (1) and (2) when he maintains (p.292) that "the particular view of the majority and of its relation to liberty" elaborated in *On Liberty* is a recurring theme throughout Mill's writings. He finds that in an early letter to Sterling and in a series of essays, beginning principally with "The Spirit of the Age" and including "Civilization", "Coleridge", the reviews of Tocqueville, and *Auguste Comte and Positivism*, Mill proceeded to undermine the eighteenth century liberal belief in the essential rationality and autonomy of the individual by arguing that the "natural state" for most men is one of "willling dependence on authority." "Mill's political theory" thus "reflects in its depths. . . the recognition that the 'individual' of classical liberalism is not the natural man and that a considerable number of men possessing political signicificance are not in fact 'individuals'. This theme in Mill's writings reaches its final expression in the essay *On Liberty.*" (p.293.)

Friedman's argument at this critical juncture becomes infuriatingly compressed. Instead of supporting his interpretation by quotation he merely cites, in a lengthy footnote (pp.292-93), passages allegedly establishing Mill had a life-long belief in "the multitude's willing submission to authority." Without exception, these passages refer to the deference of the majority to the clerisy in an organic society rather than to the conformity of the majority in a mass society. What is more, the deference is rational deference to genuine authority and so not, in Mill's view, incompatible with the autonomy and self-development of the majority. The rationale of the need for this deference is to be found in the specialized and technical nature of physical, social and moral science and the lack of leisure and education of the majority.

> "I yield to no one," Mill declares, "in the degree of intelligence of which I believe them [the majority] to be capable. But I do not believe that, along with this intelligence, they will ever have sufficient opportunities of study and experience to become themselves familiarly conversant with all the inquiries which lead to the truths by which it is good to receive into their minds the whole of the

evidence from which these truths have been collected, and which is necessary for their establishment."[33]

From this it is clear that the type of authority Mill is speaking of is the authority of the expert. The authority of those who have devoted themselves to "the investigation of physical, moral, and social truths" depends upon the fact that they alone can "be expected to make the evidences of such truths a subject of profound meditation and to make themsleves thorough masters of the philosophical grounds of those opinions of which it is desirable that all should be firmly persuaded, but which they alone can entirely and philosophically *know.*"[34] Contrary to what Friedman would have us believe, Mill is not here revising his "philosophical anthropology" or "theory of human nature" by amending the classical liberal view of men as "by nature individuals" (p.298) in favour of the view that they naturally display a "willing dependence on authority" (p.293). On Mill's view, no irreconcilable conflict arises between the conception of the authority of the expert and the notion of the autonomous individual who is both the ideal and the presupposition of liberalism. Recognition of the authority of the expert does not require that the majority should surrender their rationality and autonomous activity. From the fact that the majority ought to defer to the superior knowledge of experts it does not follow that men should not inquire and investigate; they should do so to the utmost limit of their intellectual capacity, leisure and inclination. It would never do to say to an ignorant and half-educated person that he should not "*use* his own judgment, for that he can never do too much"; what he should not do is trust entirely to his own judgment. "It is therefore," says Mill in summing up his discussion,

> "one of the necessary conditions of humanity, that the majority must either have wrong opinions, or no fixed opinions, or must place the degree of reliance warranted by *reason,* in the authority of those who have made moral and social philosophy their peculiar study. It is right that every man should attempt to understand his interest and his duty. It is right that he should follow his reason as far as his reason will carry him, and cultivate the faculty as highly as possible. But reason itself will teach most men that they must, in the last resort, fall back upon the authority of still more cultivated

---

[33] "The Spirit of the Age" in G. Himmelfarb, *op.cit.,* p.12.
[34] *Ibid.* Italics in the original.

minds, as the ultimate sanction of the convictions of their reason itself."[35]

Mill, then, is certainly not recommending the kind of deference to authority which implies a renunciation of self-determination and a willing transfer of all responsibility to social and political leaders. He is recommending the sort of rational respect for authority which comes from inevitable lack of expertise in those subjects upon which, in his opinion, the progress of mankind largely depends. That this is the type of deference he has in mind is further confirmed by his later discussion of the function of the clerisy in *August Comte and Positivism*. There he remarks that with a wide diffusion of scientific education among the people their faith in the clerisy "would not be the blind submission of dunces to men of knowledge, but the intelligent deference of those who know much, to those who know still more."[36]

It will be seen that Mill applies the notion of expertise just as much to wise counsel in matters of moral and political conduct as to specialised knowledge of the physical and social sciences. It need hardly be said that this is a contentious line of thought. Since the question is one that could not be broached within the confines of this chapter, it is fortunate that for my purpose it is not incumbent upon me to establish whether Mill is right or wrong in believing in the existence of moral experts. What I do need to show is the role of his belief in the structrure of his general doctrine concerning the function of the enlightened elite in an ideal organic society. The crucial question for my argument is whether Mill saw the deference due to the opinion of the moral expert in such a society as reasoned deference to genuine authority (expertise) or as blindly conforming obedience. I am not, of course, denying that if it could be shown there can be no moral experts, this would have serious implications for Mill's doctrine. But this would not affect the conclusion I am engaged in establishing, namely that Mill did not believe the majority were, by their intrinsic nature, limited to a servile condition devoid of individuality.

A further serious confusion issues from Friedman's belief that Mill regards the majority as naturally "low, abject., servile". Mill's supposed

---

[35] *Ibid.*, (my italics). See also "Tocqueville on Democracy in America" in Himmelfarb (ed.) *op.cit.*, pp.196-7; PPE, Book IV, ch.VII, sec.2, p.459; OL, p.124; *Auguste Comte and Positivism, op.cit.*, pp.97-98.
[36] *Auguste Comte and Positivism, op.cit.*, p.98.

doctrine of the permanent limitations of the majority is used by Friedman to explain a supposed distinction between Mill's "individualist" and his "social" justifications of liberty. The contention is that Mill's low view of the potential of the majority explains why he sometimes treats liberty (i.e. self-determination) as an "individual value" and at other times as a "social value". For the minority, according to Mill's alleged view, self-determination has individual value as a necessary condition of their own development and it also has social value as being the mainspring of "social progress" i.e. of material progress or " ' civilisation in the narrow sense' ". (p.302). For the majority, however, self-determination possesses only a social or instrumental value in that they see the self-determination of the minority as a primary cause of social viz. material progress. Thus Mill's revised conception of the capacity and potentiality of the majority can, we are asked to believe, be seen

> "to enter into the very structure of his justification of the principle of liberty. It is because of the existence of a majority who dislike liberty that the argument from social progress occupies such a prominent place in *Liberty,* and seems to stand in striking conflict with the 'individualist' justification of liberty." (p.303)

Friedman's contention is that the main concern of *Liberty* is with "the problem of securing the liberty of those few who desire it against the encroachment of the many who do not " (p.298), and Mill's special difficulty in Chapter III is that of somehow finding a means of persuading the majority to accept the autonomy of the elite. Mill's solution to this difficulty was to offer the majority a "social" justification of liberty; material progress was to be their "reward" for not interfering with the intellectual elite.

But even a cursory examination shows it to be an illusion either that the argument from social (i.e. material) progress occupies a prominent place in the second part of Chapter III of *Liberty* or that there is a striking contrast between the first and second parts of the Chapter. Mill devotes nearly eight pages (not four) to showing that individuality is a condition of self-development. Moreover, in the second part of the Chapter most of the space is taken up with arguments intended to show that the *individual self-development* of the majority depends upon absence of restraint upon the actions of the elite. In other words, Mill is here still primarily concerned with the 'individualist' justification of liberty, that is to say, with the individual progress of the majority, with progress in the sense of human improvement.

Mill begins this latter section of his argument in Chapter III by stating that it is, "in the first place", intended to show that the original, talented and developed few are models from whom the undeveloped many may learn something. Just as there is always the need for exceptional persons in order that new truths may be discovered, so there is always the need of such persons to "commence new practices, and set the examples of more enlightened conduct, and better taste and sense in human life."[37] The foremost benefit which the original are able to confer on the unoriginal "is that of opening their eyes; which being once fully done, they would have a chance of being themselves original."[38] By assaying untried opinions, by cracking the cake of custom, by striking out along new paths of life, the enlightened minority help to guide the rest of mankind towards truer views and "better forms of conduct." "The initiation of all wise or noble things comes and must come from individuals. . . . The honour and glory of the average man is that he is *capable of following that initiative;* that he can respond *internally* to wise and noble things, and be led to them *with his eyes open.*" [39]

This passage, it should be noted, is in line with the sort of rational deference to enlightened leadership elsewhere recommended by Mill. It eschews any suggestion of a servile and willing submission to the elite, allowing it no more than "freedom to point the way" towards "better modes of action, and customs more worthy of general acceptance".[40] Thus far, then, Mill's argument [41] is confined to bringing out the function of talented individuals as the mainspring of intellectual and moral progress. What is more, in the very next stage of his argument he goes on to insist that it is not merely or only the talented few who ought to be allowed freedom of tastes and pursuits. If he is to achieve any "spiritual development", any human being has the same need to indulge his own preferences and follow his own way of living.

> "The same things which are helps to one person towards the cultivation of his higher nature are hindrances to another. The same mode of life is a healthy excitement to one, keeping all his faculties of action and enjoyment in their best order, while to another it is a distracting burthen, which

---

[37] OL, p.122.
[38] *Ibid.,* p.123.
[39] OL, p.124. My italics.
[40] *Ibid.,* pp.125.
[41] *Ibid.,* pp.122-25.

suspends or crushes all internal life. Such are the differences among human beings in their sources of pleasure, their susceptibilities of pain, and the operation on them of different physical and moral agencies, that unless there is a corresponding diversity in their modes of life, they neither obtain their fair share of happiness, nor grow up to the mental moral, and aesthetic stature of which their nature is capable."[42]

In these passages, and in others one could mention, Mill is tacitly assuming that the majority cannot be altogether blind to the value of their own individual development. He is assuming that it is not impossible they may to a degree be persuaded to recognise the "highly gifted and instructed" as providing a model for their own thought and conduct. Nor does Mill, in the remaining pages of the Chapter, seriously concern himself with the promotion of material progress. Rather, he is above all concerned with elaborating his view of the supreme importance of diversity of "character and culture" for human "improvement" or "human development" and with the threat posed to it by the "despotism of custom", the "ascendancy of public opinion" and the alarming decrease in "variety of situations".

Friedman's misreading of Mill stems ultimately from a failure to appreciate Mill's overall purpose in *Liberty*. Friedman acknowledges that "the purpose of *Liberty* is to be 'equal to the politics of the future' " (p.293), but misconceives Mill's vision of the political future. Because he has confounded Mill's accounts of mass and organic societies he assumes Mill foresees the inevitable emergence of a mass organic society in which the majority will be in their "natural state of willing dependence on authority". (p.293) The basic purpose of *Liberty* then becomes that of preserving the individuality of the elite against the encroachments of the majority, and Mill's solution to his problem becomes that of persuading the majority to give an instrumental allegiance to the liberty of the elite in return for the reward of material progress.

But Mill did not believe the continuance of the trend towards a mass, organic society to be inevitable. He believed the direction of the trend could be altered by educated opinion, and conceived one of the most important parts of his mission in life to be that of helping to bring about the emergence of a new kind of society - a 'critical organic society' - i.e. one

---

[42] *Ibid.*, p.125.

which would combine the best elements of a critical period with the best elements of an organic period.⁴³ Thus Mill's chief purpose in *On Liberty* was not that of offering an instrumental justification of liberty for the majority in a mass organic society. His chief purpose was to prevent the emergence of such a society by erecting "a strong barrier of moral conviction" against "the tendency of all the changes taking place in the world. . . to strengthen society and diminish the power of the individual".⁴⁴ His aim was to help bring about a change in informed opinion which might succeed in preventing the emergence of the oppressive social uniformity characteristic of a mass organic society. Mass organic society he aimed to avoid in favour of critical organic society or individualist democracy.

---

⁴³ *Autobiography, op. cit.,* p.117.
⁴⁴ OL, pp.76-77.

CHAPTER IX

NEGATIVE LIBERALISM AND HIGH-MINDED LIBERALISM

Benthamite Liberalism

Mill's chief aim in Chapter II of *Utilitarianism* is to correct the most serious defect of Benthamite utilitarianism by distinguishing between higher and lower pleasures. The defect he seeks to correct is the most crucial weakness of Benthamite or classical liberalism. As Alasdaire MacIntyre has put it:

> "What Benthamite utilitarianism lacked, as J.S. Mill saw at once, and what liberalism by becoming utilitarian came to lack, was any critique of satisfaction. The ultimate criterion is "happiness" and "happiness" is simply that state in which people are getting what they want. There is no scope within the terms of utilitarianism for criticising their preferences. So that one seems condemned if one remains within the terms of Benthamism to say that people are satisfied if they get what they think they want."[1]

On Bentham's interpretation, the greatest happiness principle may be understood as the greatest *satisfaction* principle; satisfaction of wants as such is always good and satisfying the greatest number of wants constitutes the ultimate criterion of right and wrong. But in abandoning strict hedonism and revising the principle of utility by allowing higher pleasures to be preferable to lower, Mill thereby gave up the classical Benthamite thesis that every desire is intrinsically desirable. Those wants or satisfactions stunting or impairing the development of the higher faculties or rejected by competent judges are simply not worth seeking.

In thus conceding that satisfying the greatest number of desires does not constitute the criterion of right and wrong Mill reversed the relative weight assigned to freedom and to the greatest satisfaction principle by classical or Benthamite liberalism. In so doing he established liberalism on a sounder foundation. Bentham may most consistently be understood as

---

[1] A. MacIntyre, "Breaking the Chains of Reason," in E.P. Thompson (ed.) *Out of Apathy* (London, 1960) p.236.

meaning by "happiness" or "pleasure" not a special object of desire but simply any object of desire whatsoever.[2] So understood, the happiness or pleasure of anyone is equated with the ends he actually aims at, whatever they may happen to be. If this is Bentham's meaning, his principle of utility may be translated as: "so act as to ensure, as far as you can, that everyone gets what he wants and avoids what he is averse to in accordance with his own preferences."[3] In short, we give as many people as possible what they say they want; their wants, that is to say, are their own preferences. But, as Mill recognised when he said it matters not only what men do but what they are,[4] the principle of utility so interpreted creates a crucial difficulty for Benthamite liberalism.

Let us now consider the source of this difficulty. If we adopt Brian Barry's terminology, the essentially liberal strand in Benthamite liberalism is the view that it is only "want-regarding" principles which should be promoted by political activity.[5] Classical liberalism takes men's desires or wants as given; and the purpose of political activity is to help them gratify the desires they actually have, not to help them obtain what others think it good for them to want. Benthamism "is liberal because it invites us to take men as they are, and to aim at giving them what they want and not what we think is good for them; because it forbids our using any notion of duty to God or any conception of human nature or society made perfect as an

---

[2] See A.J. Ayer, "The principle of Utility", in *Philosophical Essays* (London, 1963) p.266; also S.R. Letwin, *op.cit.*, p.137.
[3] John Plamenatz, "The Legacy of Philosophical Radicalism", in M. Ginsberg (ed.) *Law and Opinion in England in the Twentieth Century* (London, 1959) p.33, . And see also S.R. Letwin, *op.cit.*, p.137.
[4] OL, p.117.
[5] Brian Barry, *Political Argument,* (London, 1965) p.66. Barry draws a fundamental distinction in political principles between "want-regarding" and "ideal regarding" principles. Want-regarding principles are those "which take wants as given and take account of only the amount and distribution of want-satisfaction"; ideal regarding principles "rank the satisfaction of some wants higher than the satisfaction of others even if the preferences of the persons whose wants are in question are different." (p.287) He draws attention (p.41) to the strong resemblance between this distinction and Sidgwick's division of theories into those which make the ultimate good happiness and those which make it excellence or perfection. Further, he expressly notes that Benthamite utilitarianism is a variant of the want-regarding theory, which he later goes on to equate (p.66) with classical liberalism.

excuse for bending other people to our will."⁶ At the heart of negative, Benthamite liberalism is the supposition that it is simply not our business to try to impose our ideals on other people. To quote Plamenatz again:
> "It is not our business to try to make other people better than they are or to try to bring into existence some social order which seems to us the most just or the best suited to the dignity of man. We can discover what we ought to do only by finding out what it is that people in fact want. We must look to their desires and not to any conceptions we may have of a perfected human nature or of the rights that belong to men in virtue of their humanity."⁷

On the classical liberal view, it follows that the proper duty of the state is to satisfy the desires men actually have rather than to make them good, or to promote what the government considers to be in their best interests.

A serious objection to Benthamite or classical liberalism is its misleading conception of "desire". Our desires are not the simple, biologically given data which this theory too readily assumes them to be. As Mill was never weary of pointing out, our desires or wants are created by what he calls "educational" influences, that is by social arrangements, including conscious social policy. In short, what we come to desire depends very much on what objects of desires have been and are presented to us. We can be taught to desire some things and not others, and in this way our characters can be and are changed.

We now perceive one of the implications of Mill's criticism of Benthamite liberalism for its failure to offer any critique of desires or satisfactions. If desires can be moulded by various social techniques, what objection could the Benthamite have to a ruling group so arranging society that people come to satisfy more easily the desires it has been decided they ought to have, regardless of the quality of those desires? A consistent Benthamite liberal would be logically compelled to approve of what would generally be regarded as a thoroughly illiberal society. One can readily enough conceive of a Brave-New-Worldish society where all or most members were so conditioned as to be more or less invariably contented, gratifying an uninterrupted train of desires and rarely, if ever, experiencing

---

⁶ John Plamenatz, *Man and Society* (London, 1963) Vol.II, p.13.
⁷ *Ibid.*, pp.12-13. Compare "The Legacy of Philosophical Radicalism", *op.cit.*, p.37.

any pain. Yet, as a result of their conditioning the members of this society would have been divorced from their humanity; by drugs, surgery, techniques of subliminal suggestion, etc., they would have been rendered incapable of rational choice, intellectual activity or aesthetic appreciation. Clearly, such an extremely paternalistic society would be regarded by all liberals (including probably most Benthamite liberals) as morally repugnant and illiberal. Nevertheless, Bentham's ultimate criterion of morality logically requires him to recommend such a society as morally praiseworthy. Without doubt Mill would have completely rejected a society of this kind as debasing the nature of man, revealing thereby that he attributed greater value to individuality and scope for self-development than to mere gratification of desires.

A thoroughgoing classical liberal would not only have to let into his theory the more indirect, manipulative forms of coercion, he would also be obliged to permit *direct* coercion to override liberty. To the Benthamite liberal non-interference was useful simply as a means to the gratification of desires. Leaving men free, it was thought, is generally the best way of enabling them to get what they want; liberty is justifiable on the practical or empirical ground of being conducive to the easier gratification of desires. Such an approach to the vindication of liberty runs up against the awkward difficulty of being too easily reversible. If one could produce a sound empirical argument showing more wants are satisfied by coercing people than by letting them alone then the implication is that one should accept such interference and sacrifice people's liberty.

An even more serious difficulty seems to underlie classical liberalism. Lying behind negative, or what Plamenatz calls "ordinary" liberalism, is the assumption that "it is not for other people to decide what manner of person a man should be."[8] To be sure, Plamenatz claims this is a rule which Mill and the modern or ordinary liberal share with Bentham; and Barry, too, appears to attribute this view to Mill.[9] But this is a mistake. Mill, as we have seen, had no hesitation in committing himself to elaborating and defending a specific concept of man and his essential interests; nor had he any compunction about trying to help bring into being a society in which the way of life he thought of as morally valuable might

---

[8] John Plamenatz, "The Legacy of Philosophical Radicalism", *op.cit.*, p.34.
[9] Barry, *op.cit.*, p.71, fn.

further develop and flourish. His entire programme of moral, social, and political "education" was designed to forward the cause of a humanistic liberalism. The key word in the quotation from Plamenatz is "decide". In Mill's view, it *is* for us to decide what kind of person a man should be and, where appropriate, to try to influence him by appealing to his reason, so that he will become more like that person. What we can never decide to do, though, is to employ direct coercion as a means of influencing the way we think he ought to live. Thus what Mill is objecting to in the famous "sole right" passage alluded to by Barry[10] is moral and legal "coercion", not rational persuasion. If, in our opinion, it would be better for a man, make him happier, or if it would be wise or right "there are good reasons for remonstrating with him, or reasoning with him or persuading him, or entreating him, but not for compelling him, or visiting him with any evil in case he do otherwise."[11]

Plamenatz seems rather muddled on this question. He admits one can make men and women want what you can easily give them, and agrees that the failure to notice this was a flaw in the older, Benthamite liberalism. Yet surprisingly he then goes on to contend that the modern liberal "looks askance at attempts to form the tastes and preferences of grown-up persons," the objection in which Plamenatz and the modern liberal agree being the practical one that because adults are set in their ways it is difficult to change their characters and tastes.[12] Plamenatz's considered view, however, seems to be the one we have been discussing above, namely that even when it is easier to change people's wants than to satisfy them, the "*principles*" of "the true liberal" prevent "our moulding other people to suit ourselves."[13] But this position, too, looks to be unsatisfactory. Plamenatz's brand of ordinary, negative liberalism can rule out direct coercion, i.e. prohibitions reinforced by physical sanctions. But can it forbid such indirect forms of coercion as "moulding" on any ground other than that no one has any right to intrude his own preferences on another adult? Mill can object to moulding as being incompatible with autonomy. But since Plamenatz seems to be operating solely with the negative sense of freedom - where a man is free insofar as he "gets what

---

[10] *Op.cit.*, p.71 fn.
[11] OL, p.73.
[12] John Plamenatz, "The Legacy of Philosophical Radicalism", p.37.
[13] *Ibid.*, p.36. My italics.

he wants and avoids what he is averse to in accordance with his own preferences"[14] - his only way of objecting to moulding would seem to be by invoking the principle of pure tolerance. Yet if he takes this route, resting his case against shaping the ideals of others on principle rather than practicality, how can he then consistently defend his belief about the ordinary liberal - that the liberal wants children to "acquire worthwhile tastes and ambitions" and is thus justified in using appropriate education to form their tastes and preferences?[15]

High-Minded Liberalism

By assaying a critique of wants or satisfactions Mill, in effect, abandoned classical or Benthamite liberalism in favour of what Plamenatz has called "high-minded" liberalism.[16] "A good example of the high-minded liberal is John Stuart Mill. For him the excellence of man consists above all in his capacity for self-improvement. The best man is he who has high ideals and strives valiantly to achieve them, but who, at the same time, respects the right of others to have different ideals."[17] Though he praises the high-minded liberal as being readier than the "ordinary" ('negative') liberal to defend freedom, Plamenatz betrays some uneasiness in allowing Mill's high-minded humanism to be counted an example of a genuine liberal theory. Indeed, he seems to waver on this issue, claiming there is nothing distinctively liberal about the idea of self-improvement and arguing that "what makes the liberal a liberal" is his insisting on "a man's right to pursue ends of his own choosing."[18] Evidently, Mill is to be admitted to the liberal pantheon only because he was concerned to uphold the right to non-interference. In short, Plamenatz identifies liberalism with traditional, negative liberalism and according to him it is only because Mill sets such great store by negative liberty that Mill's theory may be said to be genuinely liberal. On this matter Plamenatz is in agreement with Barry, for whom liberalism is the view that only want-regarding principles should be promoted by political action. I shall come back to this problem of the

---

[14] *Ibid.*, p.33.
[15] *Ibid.*, p.37.
[16] John Plamenatz, *Readings from Liberal Writers* (London, 1965), p.26.
[17] *Ibid.*, p.26.
[18] *Ibid.*, pp.26, 28.

definition of liberalism. The question we must now ask is: Why does Plamenatz hesitate to describe Mill's theory as liberal? The answer, it would seem, is that Mill's supreme value is self-development, not non-interference, and Plamenatz fears that stress on self-development and 'positive freedom' can very easily lead one down the slippery slide towrds paternalism in politics.[19] Here is raised in an acute form the question whether Mill's theory may properly be called liberal.

I assay an answer to that question by way of examining in some detail the views of two of Mill's most recent and most unsympathetic critics, Shirley Letwin and Maurice Cowling. Both Letwin and Cowling have argued forcefully and at length that Mill's theory is basically illiberal. If their interpretations could be sustained, my own account of Mill's liberalism would be altogether undermined. At the more general level of political principles Mill can, however, as I believe, be defended against the most damaging of the main charges brought against him. Even so, Letwin and Cowling do succeed in making out a case of some initial plausibility and in drawing attention to several unresolved (and possibly irresolvable) tensions in the fabric of Mill's attempts to apply his general principles to the resolution of some of the practical social and political problems of his own day. Some of Mill's attempts to apply his principles in dealing with these issues will be referred to in a later chapter.[20] For the most part, however, my discussion will remain at the more abstract, theoretical level on which, in the main, Letwin and Cowling rest their case against Mill.

The criticisms levelled against Mill by Letwin and Cowling are complex and various, and it would be a futile exercise to try to weld them all into a single body of objections. Both critics are, nevertheless, led to their general conclusions along routes which converge at key points, points where they can be seen to share common interpretations of several fundamental aspects of Mill's thought. It does seem possible, therefore, to pick out from the two writers (and in the process make more precise) the main charges against Mill and to consider them in turn. I consider Letwin's and Cowling's interpretation of Mill's doctrine of self-perfection and his view of the role of the elite. This discussion is followed by an examination of

---
[19] *Ibid.*, pp.27-29. See also *The English Utilitarians* (Oxford, 1958) p.178, pp.180-82.
[20] Chapter XI.

Cowling's efforts to exhibit Mill's high-minded liberalism as essentially authoritarian.

Letwin on Mill's Doctrine of Self-Perfection and the Role of the Elite

A foundation of the Letwin thesis is the observation that, despite what has usually been assumed, Mill's central concern throughout his political writings is not individual liberty, but "perfection", or "the higher cultivation". Tracing the course of Mill's intellectual history, Letwin notes how, following his mental crisis and under the influence of Coleridge and Comte, he first became enamoured of the ideas of progress and perfectibility. After the publication of *The Spirit of the Age,* he came to feel that what mattered most was progress in "personal cultivation," which then became the dominant theme in his writings. Mill set much greater store upon progress than upon liberty, the view runs. Furthermore, his theory of progress led him to look forward to a steady improvement in the state of mankind; he envisaged a succession of stages stretching forward to an ideal state of things when truth would reign supreme and the "ideal individual" would be embodied in every member of society.

In Letwin's view, the "image of the ideal individual haunts everything he [Mill] wrote."[21] As she pictures him, Mill's "ideal individual" is the man who "self-consciously chooses for himself how he will live," who "makes full use of his powers," and, though possessed of strong energies and an "active character", yet "relies on his will to make certain of his faculties dominant over the rest."[22] He appears in a number of different contexts: most plainly in the *Liberty,* especially in the chapter on individuality, but also in *Representative Government* and in *Utilitarianism* where Mill distinguishes between the higher and lower in characters as well as in pleasures.

As a result of his adherence to the ideal of perfection, a deep ambiguity opened up in Mill's liberalism. Part of his liberalism was cast in the classical, Benthamite mould: "part of him believed ardently that human

---
[21] Letwin, *op.cit.,* p.302.
[22] *Ibid.,* pp.302-4.

dignity required the freedom of each man to go his own way."[23] But another part of him could not be content with this unrestricted, entirely negative account of liberty. Mill was a man who "with one part of him genuinely values liberty and recognises the equal right of all adults to decide for themselves, but with another wants the government, under the direction of the superior few, to impose what he considers the good life on all his fellows".[24] He cared more deeply for progress than for liberty but struggled to pay homage to both without having to acknowledge any conflict between them.

In Letwin's view, the doctrine that perfection is the supreme principle of morals and politics is in Mill's thought closely linked with his aim of establishing the social and political authority of an educated and cultivated elite. The ultimate goal is the achievement of truth and perfection; this cannot be attained without the intellectual and moral overlordship of a class of educated and cultivated experts. "Mill's purpose, not only in *Utilitarianism,* but also in *On Liberty* as well as in everthing else written after his crisis was exactly contrary to Bentham's. He meant to secure the leadership of those who knew better." After that time the theme of almost all his articles "was the importance of distinguishing in politics between those who really knew and those who did not." His theory of progress had taught him the course of history made a certain class in society inherently qualified to rule. He came to believe there was "a clearly defined class of human beings", those "who knew best". These were the people who were acquainted with both 'higher' and 'lower' pleasures, were aware of the higher potentialities of men, and saw their appointed task as that of directing the course of social progress. The new intellectual and moral leaders were mainly to be sociologists, a priesthood "able to understand the true course of events, and on the basis of this information to tell people how they should live."[25]

Letwin is far from explicit about what she conceives of as the exact nature and function of the elite. She appears to think that Mill conceived of it as a political elite of "scientifically trained experts." Its primary function would, apparently, be to circumscribe the power of citizens by determining

---

[23] *Ibid.,* p.307.
[24] *Ibid.,* p.8.
[25] *Ibid.,* pp.8, 306, 307.

the details of legislation and by foisting upon them laws embodying the standards of the enlightened minority.[26] Mill proposed a legislative commission of scientific experts, to draw up laws for parliamentary approval. This institutional proposal Letwin interprets as designed to help ensure the political dominance of the class of experts. This, however, is the only concrete example she produces of a proposal of Mill's supposedly designed to promote self-perfection to the detriment of political freedom or negative liberty.

There is, nonetheless, no doubt in Letwin's mind that Mill's high valuation of perfection, coupled with his belief in the leadership of an intellectual elite, logically commits him to authoritarianism. His high-minded type of liberalism subordinates individual freedom to perfection and so provides a justification for the violation of negative freedom. His view would imply that if self-development could more easily be achieved by means of coercion, then negative freedom would lose its justification. Mill's hierarchical morality knocks down at one blow the Benthamite barriers to the use of coercion, since it enables a member of the elite "to feel it is right, even obligatory, to impose his own views on the less fortunate mass of people in want of uplifting."[27]

Unlike Maurice Cowling, Letwin does not, though, regard Mill himself as a conscious authoritarian. Her diagnosis is meant to reveal him as a schizophrenic liberal, as a man who, while embarking upon his intellectual career as an unqualified adherent of Benthamite individualism, was drawn irresistibly towards a predominately illiberal position. "Mill had poured his new learning - that there was prefection ahead - into the old mould - that it was indecent to prevent any adult from choosing his way of life. He himself managed to remain devoted to both aspects of his creed at once."[28] Letwin seems to have been too ready to cry 'Inconsistency!' here. The fact that Mill was, as she points out, able to hold both views together, makes it incumbent upon us to find a coherent and consistent account of his overall position, if possible.

---

[26] *Ibid.*, pp.250, 288-90.
[27] *Ibid.*, p.308 cf. p.252.
[28] *Ibid.*, p.308.

Expressed in terms more consonant with my own account of Mill's liberalism, the "ambiguity" in Mill's doctrine upon which Letwin is insisting is this: If one takes the view that it is in a man's permanent interests to become free, in the sense of being self-directing, is it not possible a conflict may arise between this type of freedom and freedom as the absence of constraint? We may be able to see that the sort of thing a man is doing or the kind of influences to which he is subjected are likely to damage his powers of critical judgment, weaken his will and so prevent him perfecting his powers. Is it not, then, incumbent on us to constrain him from leading the type of life he wants to lead, at the very least by protecting him from the corrupting influences of mediocre opinion and low-grade morality? Or, as Letwin puts it: "He [Mill] provided a justification for withholding personal liberty from any claimant unable to demonstrate that he was pursuing the 'right' ideal and was possessed of sufficient will power to pursue it steadily and energetically."[29]

But this passage reveals a crucial failure on Letwin's part to enter sympathetically into Mill's scheme of values. For it suggests Mill believed the "right" ideal could be promoted by coercion. Letwin sees clearly enough that Mill was operating with two distinct ideals which, in certain circumstances, might easily conflict. One of these, as she notes, is that of non-interference - liberty understood as the absence of external constraint. The other ideal she identifies as that of "perfection" or "progress" (i.e. progress towards perfection), and it is precisely here that her thesis begins to miss the mark. At one point she does give an account of Mill's "ideal individual" which reveals him as essentially self-determining. Yet in her argument she does not take account of the fact that for Mill self-determination is both a necessary means to and a vital part of self-perfection, so that self-determination always *requires* non-interference.

It will be recalled that the core of Mill's position as I have presented it is: (i) Perfection is largely *self*-perfection, i.e. our capacities are improved only by being exercised. Thus we must rely mainly upon our own inner forces if we are to develop our higher powers. (ii) Hence autonomy, or self-determination, is possible only if the state and society do not interfere with or constrain us over a certain range of our activities (which Mill attempts to

---

[29] *Ibid.*, p.308.

delimit): the development of a man's higher capacities requires self-activity - the exercise of judgment and the movement of the will. If a person's range of choice is restricted because the area within which he is allowed to choose freely is eaten into by oppressive controls, his opportunities for developing his higher potentialities are to that extent diminished. (iii) The ability to be self-directing requires social diversity, the existence of a considerable range of ways of living from which we can select those best suited to our own individual character and style of thought. This again involves toleration or non-interference on the part of state and society. (iv) Finally, on Mill's view, non-interference is an important good in its own right. For him "all restraint *qua* restraint is an evil." If people are prevented from doing what they have a desire to do or made to do what they do not want to do, they experience a sense of frustration more or less according to the strength of their desire.[30] And, on the other hand, of course, if left free to satisfy their impulses they are able to enjoy a feeling of spontaneity.

Letwin's argument is that if self-perfection can be achieved more successfully through coercion then non-interference loses its *raison d'etre*. But in Mill's conception of the good life self-determination is a *necessary component* of self-perfection and non-interference is a *necessary condition* of self-determination. It is true that Mill's central concern is self-development and that he thinks that it is in the best interests of men and women to devote themselves to worthwhile activities. But then according to Mill's doctrine it is generally not possible to promote their self-development by trying to force them to engage in worthwhile pursuits or by protecting them from the influence of corrupting opinions or conduct. In general, he does not believe it possible to coerce people into leading the good life: even though external conditions may help or hinder the process, in the final resort, men and women can only be induced to lead the good life if they are persuaded by rational arguments, if they are given and are convinced by good reasons.

---

[30] OL, pp.150, 569. PPE, Book V, Chapter XI, Sec.2, p.569.

Political Paternalism

Mill is strongly opposed to any form of paternalism because paternalism involves protection, and protection means that the community is divided into protectors and the protected: it means treating adults as children and so hindering them from developing their potentialities. By protecting individuals from what are considered morally dangerous opinions or practices or by imposing on them, in their own interests, certain forms of behaviour or moral standards, paternalism involves constraint, and constraint removes the possibility of free choice, thereby weakening intellect and character, and making it much too difficult for people to develop the ability to think and act on their own initiative.

At this point it might easily be objected that there can, in principle, be no absolute bar to constraining others for their own good, since we clearly do not believe paternalism to be inappropriate when dealing with children. To this objection Mill is quite ready to agree, but with the proviso that the relevant difference between children and adults is critical. His doctrine of self-protection, he hastens to admit, does not apply to children, young persons or adults in societies so backward that they impose limitations leaving little or no room for the application of the idea of spontaneous self-development. "Those who are still in a state to require being taken care of by others must be protected against their own actions as well as against external injury."[31] Mature adults have already benefitted from education and experience and hence may be presumed to be capable of profiting from intellectual argument and rational discussion. By contrast, the higher faculties of children and savages are at an incipient stage of development, so they are neither very susceptible to rational persuasion nor capable of discerning that their long-term interests are best served by submitting themselves to the regimen of a course of instruction or a period of political apprenticeship. Mill considers the situation of children in the sphere of education: he sees a certain amount of discipline and compulsion as obviously necessary if they are to acquire the intellectual equipment and moral sense of even the average adult. They must, therefore, first be compelled to attend school and, once there, must be trained in self-control and obedience if they are to learn anything of the subjects being taught.

---

[31] OL, p.73.

For this reason he was strongly in favour of compulsory, elementary education even though it included constraints upon children as well as interference with what was then regarded as a sacred right of parents.

What is of special significance about the cases of children and backward peoples, however, is that it brings out his *general opposition* to political paternalism. Far from its being the case (as Letwin wishes to suggest) that Mill is concerned to perpetuate the leadership of a paternalistic elite, his treatment of the cases of children and "barbarians" indicates that this is precisely what he is striving to avoid. For he sees the *purpose* of both education and political apprenticeship as the elimination of exactly those deficiencies of intellect and character which justify paternalism. In reply to the likely objection that in compelling children to attend school for their own good he is being paternalistic, Mill's rejoinder is that suitable instruction "strengthens as well as enlarges the active faculties" and favours the spirit of independence: it is designed to overcome the need for discipline and compulsion by providing "help towards doing without help."[32] Similarly, in discussing the government of backward countries Mill insists that the object of the ruler should always be to train the people to become free, self-governing citizens. For, "as soon as mankind have attained the capacity of being guided to their own improvement by conviction or persuasion (a period long since reached in all nations with whom we need here concern ourselves), compulsion, either in the direct form or in that of pains and penalties for non-compliance, is no longer admissible as a means to their own good, and justifiable only for the security of others."[33]

The Essay on Liberty
and the Domination of the Elite

Letwin's principal charge against Mill, I have argued, rests on a failure to appreciate that, in Mill's view, self-perfection involves self-determination and so rules out coercion. A supporter of Mill could, in any case, adopt a further line of defence. He might agree on there being two sides to Mill's view of liberty and admit the possibility of tension arising

---
[32] PPE, Book V, Chapter XI, Sec.8, p.576.
[33] OL, pp.73-74.

between them. He might also concede that Mill's vision of social progress depends upon the existence and authority of a superior elite. Yet he might still wish to argue that Mill himself was scarcely if ever tempted by authoritarianism. After all, he might say, it has not been shown that when Mill's two ideals do conflict he always, or even sometimes, comes down on the side of self-perfection at the expense of non-interference. Surely, the supporter might conclude, Mill's principle of self-protection as enunciated in *On Liberty* puts his general attitude beyond doubt. For that principle lays it down that coercion is justified only if actions damage the interests of others.

In order to meet this possible rejoinder, Letwin finds it necessary to subject *On Liberty* to a radical reinterpretation. *On Liberty,* she argues, is not designed to promote negative freedom for all; it is concerned to restrict the freedom of the many in order to protect that of the elite.

At a first reading, Letwin concedes, *On Liberty* does look like an ardent and persuasive argument for the most unhindered individualism. This is undoubtedly the way in which it has traditionally been understood and there are, she thinks, some grounds for such an interpretation. Some of its arguments are obviously in the Benthamite mode: Mill pleads for liberty as a dictate of utility; he makes considerable play with the Benthamite argument that each individual is necessarily the best judge of his own interests; and, above all, he lays down the principle that the individual is not accountable to society for his actions insofar as they concern no one but himself. By having recourse to arguments such as these, says Letwin, Mill gave his readers to understand he was assaying a classic defence of individualism.

Yet had they stopped to look even a little way beneath the surface of the essay they must have detected a vindication of an individualism very different from Bentham's. For though Mill appeared to be appealing simply for the liberty of the individual, his ulterior purpose was to secure the freedom of the "ideal individual", and in order to do this it was necessary to "free the superior few from the vulgar many". Hence "his reason for fostering individuality was not any simple objection to letting one man impose his will on another" but rather to persuade ordinary men and women that the superior individuals must be exempted from the external controls of popular morality. When, for instance, Mill affirms that if a person is to be free he must throw off the sway of custom and tradition, he should be understood as referring not to the mass of ordinary people but only to the men of education and genius, whose freedom is necessary in order that they may be able to goad, guide and serve as a model to the rest. Custom and tradition are, after all, part of popular morality and, so Letwin argues, Mill was too shrewd not to be aware that most men and women find these indispensable. Mill is all along assuming, Letwin thinks, that there are in society two distinct classes - the elite and the "mass of ordinary human beings". Corresponding to these classes are two moralities: the higher morality and the popular morality. The "best popular morality is that which pacifies as many natures as possible, and so it must be inferior to what higher natures want and require". And "the purpose of *On Liberty,*" it transpires, "was not to insist on the priority of liberty over morality, but on the priority of the higher over the lower morality." If the leadership of the minority of ideal individuals was in this way made secure, then in the long run the common herd would become capable of high thought and elevated feelings, but in the mean time, it was essential to free the enlightened from the confines of the morality of the benighted masses. Mill's chief purpose in his famous essay was really to free the elite from the external controls "properly binding on the majority". That this has been almost entirely overlooked is, Letwin thinks, due to the fact that his "plea for freeing the superior few from the inferior mass was so sweetly enclosed in general arguments for liberty and individuality that it could be accepted somehow by all sorts of individualists." Concluding her reinterpretation of the essay, Letwin epitomises it as "a classic statement of late Victorian and twentieth century liberalism;" it "enables the liberal to feel assured of his tolerance, and at the same time to feel it right, even obligatory, to impose his own views on the less fortunate mass of people in want of uplifting."[34]

Such an essentially paternalistic and conservative view cannot fairly be attributed to Mill. My own account of *On Liberty* emphasized that even if he thought of individuality as dispersed throughout society, he realised that it was much more developed in some persons than in others. Thus if the adult members of advanced societies were to be placed along an individuality continuum, the majority would be found clustered at one end. Nevertheless, he did not conclude they were, therefore, unfit for liberty and

---

[34] The preceding quotations from Letwin's argument are from Letwin, *op.cit.,* pp.300-1, pp.306-7.

that progress depended largely on their being prevented from putting obstacles in the path of the advanced minority. If the freedom of the intellectual and moral elite at the expense of the many, means that the many are to be restrained by custom and tradition and by the rules and conventions of popular morality, while the few do not need to be so shackled, then Mill did not believe in this. Letwin's interpretation on this point is, if we stop to think about it, obviously incoherent and bordering on the absurd. For (as she concedes elsewhere) the long-term goal for Mill's liberalism is that *all* individuals should become more like the talented and exceptional few, in being freer of the restrictions of conventional morality. For him, this is what social progress consists in. It hardly seems likely, then, that Mill should have supposed the best way of attaining that end was to persuade the masses the "lower morality" was suitable for them, but unsuitable for the gifted few.

Maurice Cowling also denies that *On Liberty* is designed to promote an unqualified liberty. He grants that on a superficial reading the essay may be judged libertarian. But he thinks that if it can be established that Mill's much vaunted principle of individuality "includes less than all the ends to which men might want to move" then the principle is "designed to detract from human freedom, not to maximise it."[35] This, he believes, can in fact be established if one brings out the real import of Mill's principle of self-protection. That principle stipulates any interference with a man's conduct is unjustified unless his action injure the interests of others. But Mill has in mind here, according to Cowling, not a person's interest in the subjective, "vulgar selfish sense", but his objective interest, "his interest as a progressive being" - a being who has an obligation to pursue the higher cultivation and to be concerned for the well-being of society as a whole. Further, it is obvious Mill will not regard men as acting in their 'progressive' interests if they are selfish or gratify their sensual natures at the expense of their higher capacities. Or if they decline to be educated, remain unwilling to "be persuaded to the rational conclusions enjoined by their higher natures" or refuse to defer to the authority of the clerisy. From this it follows, Cowling thinks, that if the chief end is to further man's "interest as a progressive being" then interference with individual freedom will be justified if it serves to promote those interests. "For, if interference with

---

[35] Cowling, *op.cit.*, p.98.

individual freedom can be justified on the ground that interference is in the interest of others, and if the interest of others is taken to lie in producing the greatest amount of higher happiness possible", then "individuality is likely to flourish only as long as it is connected with the higher cultivation of the sentiments."[36]

Cowling is then, however, forced to concede that Mill's principle of self-protection rules out interference with individual freedom except in cases where there is assignable damage to the interests of others. And this, he has to admit, might seem to make Mill's principle more libertarian than his (Cowling's) argument would allow. For Mill's principle would certainly appear to prohibit the use of force as a means of *promoting* people's interests and confine its use to circumstances in which their actions adversely affect the interests of others.

But we must now ask, Cowing contends, *why* Mill allows liberty to be absolute in circumstances where no definite damage is done to the interests of others. Mill's answer is said to reveal his individualism to be far more restrictive than it would appear. For he allows so much liberty *not* because he favours individuality as such but because he regards it as a necessary condition of the attainment of the "higher happiness". He was in favour of non-interference simply because he thought the higher cultivation is more likely to be maximised "by allowing full individual liberty, than by preventing the damage a free man may do by perversely misusing his freedom."[37]

John Rees[38] has drawn attention to an inconsistency in Cowling's argument at this point. Cowling begins his reassessment of *On Liberty* by denying the libertarian character of Mill's liberalism on the grounds that he would condone interference if it could be shown to promote the interests (that is to say further the self-perfection) of other people. Yet he is then obliged to admit that Mill is in principle against interfering with people for their own good. Cowling is thus, in effect, disowning his original point, namely that Mill's principle of self-protection is designed to promote men's

---
[36] *Ibid.*, p.100. Cowling's italics.
[37] *Ibid.*, p.102.
[38] In "Was Mill for Liberty?", *Political Studies*, Vol.XIV, October, 1966, pp.72-77.

'objective' interests by forcing them into a disinterested pursuit of the higher cultivation.

I question, though, whether too much should be made of this particular slip on Cowling's part. For the thesis he otherwise consistently maintains is that Mill saw his liberalism as achieving its success by means of persuasion and education rather than by coercive interference. He is, in general, insisting that individual liberty is to Mill merely instrumental; it is valued simply on the ground that a free man is more likely than an unfree one to achieve the higher happiness. Cowling's reinterpretation of *On Liberty* then runs as follows. If men are freed from "mediocre social pressure", it will become possible for them "to reflect on, and choose, the right action rather than the wrong one." Once the oppressive moral consensus of mediocre opinion, habit and custom has been removed, it will be replaced by a better consensus, one that will arise naturally as an outcome of the system of rational education provided by the clerisy. The way to bring about such rational consensus in society is not to try to impose it by coercive measures, but "to leave men's minds absolutely open to the working of rational education - because it is only through rational education that unforced assent to the right means of determining the right course of action will take root."[39]

Mill's central purpose in *On Liberty*, Cowling is in general arguing, was to free men from the sway of custom and popular morality so that society might approach as closely as possible to a condition in which its members would be "seekers after a cultivated disinterestedness of character and cultivated elevation of mind."[40] Thus Mill's central purpose is not "libertarian" or "simply individualistic", for he is not concerned to free men from the domination of any and every kind of doctrine but merely from the control of custom, habit and mediocre public opinion.

> "*On Liberty*. . . so far from being an attempt to free men from the impositions of *all* doctrine, is an attempt to free them from customary, habitual, conventional doctrine. Convention, custom and the mediocrity of opinion are the enemies in Mill's mythology: the freedom he gives is given in order to subject men's prejudices to reasoning authority. *On Liberty* does not offer safeguards for *individuality;* it is designed to

---
[39] *Ibid.,* p.103.
[40] *Ibid.,* p.51.

propagate the individuality of the elevated by protecting *them* against the mediocrity of opinion as a whole."[41]

On Liberty is illiberal, Cowling is saying, because it does not treat non-interference, or diversity in and for itself, as the highest good. Once men have been freed from the mediocre consensus imposed on them by custom, habit and convention, then a better consensus - Mill's own brand of higher liberalism - is to replace it. Mill's "purpose in allowing men liberty, the justification of individuality, is not diversity in itself, but diversity informed by the rationally agreed education the clerisy alone can provide."[42] Thus the individuality which Mill wished to see prosper was to be confined within the bounds set by his doctrine of disinterested cultivation and to be developed under the guidance and authority of the clerisy.

Though Cowling emphasises that Mill's main aim in *On Liberty* was to "protect the elite from domination by mediocrity", he is not, of course, claiming (as Letwin does, though not consistently) that Mill wishes to keep the majority in a state in which they continue to live according to the dictates of popular morality. Cowling is not quite explicit, but his position seems to be something like this: The clerisy, who have already accepted the liberal-utilitarian ethic, must remain free from the pressure of irrational and prejudiced opinion if they are to forward their programme of educational indoctrination. But the rest of society must also, as far as possible, be freed of mediocre opinion if they are to make an approach to the kind of critical reflection and reasoning which will induce them to embrace liberal-utilitarianism. Mill, Cowling states, is here thinking not merely of the educated and cultivated classes but of all and sundry. "All men, whatever their class, temperament or social standing" are capable of making the approach to the life of self-conscious, critical reflection. Mill is "saying that all men have an obligation, and once they have been educated, have the opportunity, to submit their own and society's actions, to rational questioning."[43] Mill, Cowling is pointing out, wishes to move towards a society in which all men, including those at present ignorant and uneducated, will succeed in attaining a certain educational level and in possessing a certain degree of critical ability. This, Cowling thinks, will be a

---
[41] *Ibid.*, p.104. Cowling's italics.
[42] *Ibid.*, pp.104-5.
[43] *Ibid.*, p.29.

level at which they are sufficiently rational to defer to the superior wisdom and morality of the clerisy, and also are able to arrive (by rational reflection) at proper conclusions concerning the true end of life and the correct means of attaining it.

Is Liberalism Essentially Authoritarian?

Cowling believes Mill's liberalism to be authoritarian because it subordinates the value of non-interference to that of the pursuit of a rational and disinterested perfection. But he is then obliged to admit that Mill looks to "rational education," not to legal or social coercion, to promote the higher cultivation. Yet he continues to insist that Mill's view is illiberal, even authoritarian! Now this seems very odd indeed, since Mill's programme of persuasion by rational argument is customarily taken to be the very paradigm of liberalism. This brings us to the root of Cowling's objection to Mill's liberalism. What lies behind his objection emerges once one realizes that, for him, Mill's liberalism is not simply and as a matter of fact authoritarian, it is *necessarily* so.

In Cowling's view, Mill's liberalism is necessarily authoritarian because it rests upon a gross misconception of the true nature of morality.[44] Cowling is convinced there is no way in which Mill can possibly establish that commitment to one way of life is any more reasonable than commitment to another. It follows that commitment to the critical reflection, moral questioning and aesthetic activity which Mill associates with general cultivation cannot on principle be shown to be any more reasonable than, say, a life devoted to pushpin and the satisfaction of "the instincts or animal feelings". It now begins to emerge that, lying behind Cowling's critique, is a fundamental doctrine of his own concerning the possibility of moral and political justification. Confirmation that this is so is to be found by focussing attention on his examination of Mill's account of the nature of liberal education.

---

[44] See D.H. Munro's review of Cowling's book in *The Australasian Journal of Philosophy,* Vol.42, 1964.

Cowling, in a number of places, points out that Mill never contemplates the clerisy having to use force in order to establish the authority of their liberalism. The liberal point of view in Mill's scheme of things, is to be established entirely by means of educative rational persuasion. How, then, one might object, can it seriously be called 'authoritarian'? Surely, the contrast between rational persuasion at one end of the scale of influence and naked coercion at the other, is a fundamental pre-supposition of liberalism? True, there may be ticklish problems about where the line is to be drawn here. Yet it can hardly be doubted that whereas naked coercion is clearly not compatible with autonomy, rational persuasion clearly is compatible. If a man is persuaded by rational argument to believe something or do something we do not ordinarily consider him to be acting under constraint. We normally draw a sharp distinction between force of argument and force of arms. Where we are convinced by force of argument, the argument does 'compel' us in the sense that it is the means of securing our agreement, but this is only a weak and non-literal sense of 'compulsion'. What is left out is just what, in ordinary as opposed to Cowling's English, is taken to be essential to literal compulsion, namely the use or threat of a sanction, a punishment associated with non-agreement or non-compliance.

I have earlier called manipulation a more subtle form of coercion, so it is now incumbent on me to relate manipulation to the distinction between naked force and force of argument. Manipulation resembles naked force and differs from force of argument in the respect relevant to my overall discussion of liberalism. The relevant matter is that when agreement is secured either by naked force or by manipulation the particular means of securing agreement is logically irrelevant to what is agreed to (does not bear on it either as argument or as evidence); it is involved in the decision to agree only because it has been introduced for the purpose of securing agreement. Whether the (logically!) irrelevant means of securing our agreement is a gun barrel or, say, a subliminal advertisement's promise of sexual adventure, there is a common objectionable element in the persuader's use of the irrelevant means. What is objectionable is the failure to respect in the person so persuaded his individuality, his being an autonomous source of reasoning and decision. In both naked force and manipulation those who are made to comply are used as extensions of the will of another. Naked force and manipulation therefore resemble one another, differing mainly in the degree of difficulty involved in offering resistance to them, whereas force of argument is different in character from either. And because of the characteristic difference I have drawn attention to, naked force and manipulation are illiberal whereas the use of argument to convince some one shows a liberal respect for him as an autonomous source of reasoning.

Cowling wishes to obliterate this distinction. It sometimes seems that he wants to obliterate it as it applies to the force of argument quite generally; but what is apposite to my discussion is that there can be no doubt he wants to obliterate it as it applies to the force of argument offered in justification of moral and political policies. In this area, rational persuasion or rational argument is to him no more than a form of "moral indoctrination". He writes:

> "It is the business of the clerisy, a function of the intellectual 'elite', to provide (through general culture and education) a systematic indoctrination with a view to freeing men from the habitual arbitrariness which prevents them seeing their social duties for what they are."[45]

Cowling's meaning becomes plain when one turns to his interpretation of Mill's idea of a university. "Mill", he roundly declares, "supposed indoctrination to be a chief function of a university."[46] Universities were to fulfil their function by providing general culture.

> "General Culture, however, for Mill, does not mean learning to be cultivated in the accomplishments of the society in which an undergraduate is growing up (with a view to improving cultivation in the future). General Culture means, on the contrary, critical reflection and mental doubt, sceptical scrutiny of existing habits, and, where habits are judged to be irrational or wrong, deciding which habits should replace them. It means *following the argument whithersoever it leads us;* it means subjecting all conduct to critical scrutiny, and it mean rejecting assumptions which halt argument before argument gets wherever it should take us. It means, in short, moral indoctrination of a kind which would lead to the acceptance of liberal-utilitarianism."[47]

It is scarcely surprising to find Cowling arriving at this paradoxical conclusion since the point of departure for his onslaught on Mill is revealed to be a very thoroughgoing moral subjectivism indeed. His own radical

---

[45] Cowling, *op.cit.*, p.38.
[46] *Ibid.*, p.113.
[47] *Ibid.*, pp.116-17. Cowling's italics.

relativism and subjectivism while hinted at occasionally, is not stated explicitly until near the end of his book. There he makes it plain that, for him, there is no special reason why, in moral questions, rational argument and the appeal to principles should be preferred to reliance upon intuition, custom, or prejudice. To him, "Commitment is the significant word, whether men *have committed themselves* or found themselves committed."[48] There is held to be no distinction between autonomous commitment and being forced or led by the nose to co-operate. As for the question of whether one commitment is more adequate than another, that is a matter which simply cannot be resolved by philosophical argument.

> "Argument to resolve the question - which commitment should I accept? - has procedures of its own, but philosophy cannot conduct them. One set of binding commitments excludes any other: different men hold different opinions with equal certainty, and *philosophical* resolution of the conflict is impossible. These facts require the heaviest emphasis it is possible to give: a philosopher who grasps their significance will not fail to give it."[49]

Cowling's type of subjectivism has its own well-known difficulties which need not concern us here. Suffice it for my purpose to mention, in passing and *ad hominem,* that if Cowling takes himself to have established that Mill gives us no *reason* for being liberals, (since this is a decision to which reasons do not apply so that none *could* be given) then he cannot in consistency take himself to have given us a *reason* for *rejecting* liberalism. In his own terms, all discussion of liberalism either by himself or by Mill has the status of an attempt to manipulate so as to win support for one's own stance. It would indeed follow that if it is the case, as Cowling says, that reasons cannot be given for what behavioural commitments we should accept, then there is no reason we should take an interest in *that.* To be concerned about whether what Cowling says is true or not is a behavioural commitment and on his own showing, no reasons can be given for making or eschewing it.

On Mill's showing, of course, matters are quite otherwise. Cowling poses a fundamental problem for Mill's liberalism, a liberalism based upon the presupposition that the living of the good life is impossible without the absence of constraint. It assumes that coercion nullifies moral goodness by

---

[48] *Ibid.,* p.139. Cowling's italics.
[49] *Ibid.,* p.148. Cowling's italics.

removing the possibility of choice. Men must in general be "guided to their own improvement by conviction or persuasion. . ." [50] Moreover, a liberal theory, if it is to appeal to men's reason and not to mere intuition or arbitrary impulse, must itself be susceptible of some sort of philosophical justifcation. But if Cowling is right, none of this is possible. Mill's programme of improvement through rational persuasion is itself merely a conditioning process. The only way to account for its influence is to say that it is a form of indoctrination akin to that employed by political propagandists or advertisers; instead of depending for its success on an appeal to reasons, it relies upon the manipulation of impulses and the appeal to prejudice. No further effort will remedy this situation, since philosophical justification of a political doctrine is, it is alleged, strictly impossible. If Cowling's position could be sustained, then Mill's 'liberalism' would, of necessity, be authoritarian.

The difficulty Cowling poses could be fully overcome only if it were possible to show that, despite what he says to the contrary, liberalism can in fact be justified. Such a justification would depend on the possibility of an appeal to principles supported by reasons. As we saw in Chapter VII, this is exactly what Mill professes to be able to do in *Utilitarianism.* The form of justification he there invokes makes appeal to the principle that virtue is knowledge. He presupposes that once men have really understood the true nature of the activities making up the life of self-development, they will be committed to pursuing them. The final link Mill is drawing attention to is psychological, not logical, but this is not surprising given that it is reasons for *acting* that are in question. In contradiction to Cowling, I point out that far from its being the case that *no* reasons can be given for an action, the notion of having a reason is built into the notion of acting. A definitional distinction between an action and a movement may be said to be the relevance to the former but not to the latter of the questions ' Why did he do it? What reason did he have to do it? What was he up to?' over and above the question ' What caused him to do it?' The possibility of asking a man's reasons for acting presupposes that at least some community of human response by way of policy decision may be expected to issue from common beliefs about the situations in which men find themselves. In the light of this observation, the nature of Mill's justification of liberalism becomes clearer.

---

[50] OL, p.73.

He does not say the assertion 'This is intellectual activity' implies as its logical conclusion the imperative 'This ought to be pursued'. But he does claim that the person who really understands what intellectual activity is all about feels a strong and natural inclination to continue to engage in it. He claims that to say with full understanding that the following up of a certain enquiry, say, is likely to further human knowledge, is to give a *reason* for following it up. By reason here is not meant premise implying logical conclusion, but reason in the way we ordinarily intend when we explain why we did something. To say that in such a context the notion of giving a reason makes no sense is to stipulate the abandonment of our ordinary way of talking, and without substituting any new more coherent way of making the distinctions we are accustomed to make, at that.

Of course it is one thing to say that it is both comprehensible and sensible to call this a 'reason' and another to claim that it is a conclusive reason. Mill's claim is that it is a good reason and will be seen to be so by all who really understand it. But it follows from what I have been saying that if he is wrong in his assumption of the 'natural' goodness of man, then this claim fails. If, for example, even given hypothetical conditions of maximized educational opportunity, some men would reject intellectual activity, Mill is simply wrong about the nature of men and of intellectual activity and their relation. Here, though, I might be taken to be saying Mill is making an (unsupported) empirical claim. I think this is not the case. If it were, then we should have to recognise the (logical) possibility of finding a disconfirming case of someone who under conditions of maximized educational opportunity, rejected intellectual activity. Whereas it seems clear that on the contrary wherever Mill found a case of someone rejecting intellectual activity, he would say that there had been something wrong with his educational opportunities. No, the status of Mill's claim that good reasons for acting in a certain way can be given by reference to intellectuality or more broadly by reference to individuality or autonomous self-development, is not the status of an empirical claim. Rather, in what he has to say about individuality or autonomous self-development Mill claims to have uncovered the underlying rationale of our giving of reasons for acting. Appeal to the principle of autonomous self-development can never be the giving of a bad reason, because this is, as it were, the underlying appeal that we make in giving reasons for acting, or at least in correlating our reasons for different actions. What, then, would it be like to deny Mill's claim? It would be to put ourselves, in relation to a claim about the rationale of giving reasons for acting, in a position that is the analogue of denying, in the area of study of arguments having categorical components, what someone claims is a law of logic. But to rebut the claim in logic we should, notoriously, have recourse to logical considerations. We can argue about one 'law' of logic at a time, but not, as it were, all at once. To try to rebut Mill's claim in Cowling's way is to put oneself in a position that has as its analogue in logic the man who says 'There is no logic'. It is to deny what is patently true, namely that we can give reasons for acting. While it is possible to contest, by making reference to the reasons and kinds of reasons we do give, Mill's claim about the rationale of our reason-giving, it is not possible to contest it by denying the validity of reason-giving altogether. To do this is not to take issue with Mill, but to opt out of the argument. One might guess too, that such a position taken seriously would mean, psychologically speaking, opting out of action altogether. But this last is an *ad hominem* argument and by way of an aside.

CHAPTER X

THE SCOPE AND LIMITS OF LIBERTY

Pluralistic Liberalism

Historically, no doubt, political theories of rather various forms have all attracted the title 'liberal'. Still, whatever its form, "the essence of liberalism" has been "its deep concern for individual liberty".[1] Mill's theory has, of course, a very strong historical claim to be called liberal; but this, it might be said, is only because Mill is commonly thought of simply as a 'negative' liberal. Plamenatz contends (and Letwin and Cowling would clearly agree with him) that there is nothing distinctively liberal about such notions as self-development, the realization of potentialities, self-perfection. But, as I indicated earlier, in the case of Mill's account of self-development this is simply untrue. To be sure, Mill places the very highest value on self-development. At the same time, though, non-interference and self determination are valued both in and for themselves and especially because of their very close connection with self-development. Self-development, is *self-* development, that is to say it is largely a matter of self-activity, so that self-determination is the most essential prerequisite of self-development. Further, to be capable of self-determination is part of what it means to be self-developed; or, to put it in another way, the capacity for free decision is a necessary element of the developed self. And free choice requires the absence of 'external' constraints. It follows that there is the closest sort of interconnection between the three notions of non-interference, self-determination and self-development.

Utilitarianism presupposes a single, overriding moral principle, the principle of the greatest happiness. Yet Mill has argued that certain ends other than happiness, while originally desired for the pleasure accompnaying them, come in time to be desired for their own sake. He allows there are a number of goods either intrinsically valuable or valuable as means to or as essential parts of goods other than happiness; they

---
[1] H.J. McCloskey, "The Problem of Liberalism", *op.cit.,* p.249.

include self-development; justice; security; virtue; self-determination; non-interference; knowledge; progress; rational and lively belief; social diversity. In a word, Mill's liberalism is pluralistic: he recognises and tries to take account of the relevance and intrinsic worth of a variety of principles other than happiness. Furthermore, he concedes that in practice these principles may clash and allows that serious problems arise as to how we are to resolve such conflicts. Faced with the difficulty of reconciling conflicts between competing goods, Mill would have recourse to the principle of utility. But this move has the effect of retracting his admission that there are determinants of value other than happiness. In short, he tries to have things both ways. On the one hand, the logic of his liberalism forces him to allow the existence of principles independent of that of the greatest happiness. On the other hand, he does not wish to surrender the belief that all values can somehow be reduced to the single, overriding principle of utility.

Why, we may ask, does Mill draw back from a thoroughgoing pluralism which would admit the existence of diverse moral principles? His primary reason is that unless all the various things which we value can be brought under the single concept of pleasure or happiness there can never be any rational way of choosing between them in cases of conflict. One of the great advantages of Utilitarianism over Intuitionism, he thought, was that while the Utilitarian could, the Intuitionist could not show how it is possible to make a rational choice in circumstances where our intuitions yield conflicting obligations.[2] Like Bentham, Mill thinks we can make a rational choice between competing ends only if there is a common denominator - pleasure or happinesss - in terms of which the competing ends can be compared. Hence he thinks it necessary to try to subsume all our "secondary ends" under the unitary notion of the happiness of all sentient beings.

The ultimate principle of morality, Mill believes, is so abstract that it does not require to be used except where two secondary moral principles come into conflict. What the greatest happiness principle does is to provide a rational basis for testing secondary rules; its main function is not that of prescribing where our obligations lie in particular cases. This is as much as to say that Mill is a rule-utilitarian. Much more would need to be said in

---

[2] U, p.3.

order to defend this interpretation; I do not propose to undertake this task, but rather shall simply state that Mill's position does appear to be that of a rule-utilitarian. The rule-utilitarian interpretation is supported by what he says at the end of Chapter II of *Utilitarianism*. Employing the phrases "secondary principle" and "subordinate principle" to cover such rules as have been justified by some fundamental criterion, Mill maintains:

> "Whatever we adopt as the fundamental principle of morality, we require subordinate principles to apply it by; the impossibility of doing without them, being common to all systems, can afford no argument against any one in particular".

And on the following page he continues:

> "We must remember that only in these cases of conflict between secondary principles is it requisite that first priniples should be appealed to. There is no case of moral obligation in which some secondary principle is not involved. . ."[3]

Despite Mill's implicit admissions to the contrary, however, there is never any question of an explicit espousal of the view that a secondary principle could come into conflict with the supreme principle of morality.

The point I wish to take up in more detail is Mill's insistence that, unless all secondary principles can in some manner be reduced to the greatest happiness principle, any choice between competing secondary principles is bound to be irrational. He wrote:

> "There must be some standard by which to determine the goodness or badness, absolute and comparative, of ends or objects of desire. And whatever that standard is, there can be but one: for if there were several ultimate principles of conduct, the same conduct might be approved by one of those principles and condemned by another; and there would be needed some more general principle as umpire between them".[4]

Now I have earlier committed myself to the view that there can be no success in reducing all principles of moral value to the single, commensurable notion of quantity of happiness or pleasure. If this be acknowledged, how are we to find a rational way of resolving conflicts between independent principles of value? What can do the job it was intended by Mill his overriding moral principle should do? It can hardly be pretended there is an easy or obvious answer to this question. The issue is complex and would require extended discussion far behind the purview of

---

[3] *Ibid.*, pp.23, 24.
[4] *A System of Logic, op.cit.*, pp.620-21.

this chapter. All I can do is to suggest the lines which I believe a convincing answer might take and there let the matter rest.

The situation I am assuming is the ordinary or everyday one where we are faced with a plurality of distinct, absolutely irreducible principles, some of which are in conflict with one another. When this happens we cannot avoid 'weighing' or 'balancing' (in some metaphorical sense) those principles against each other. Certainly, this process of balancing is not and cannot be mathematically precise since the values involved cannot be quantified. Still, this scarcely appears a decisive objection, for the account in terms of 'balancing' does seem to correspond fairly closely to the actual ways in which disputes about clashing principles are resolved. As it has recently been put: "The thing has to be done, else much reasoning is at a stand; so it is done; so it can be done".[5] Admittedly this still leaves the weighing process a somewhat mysterious affair. A pluralistic theory claims there just are a variety of distinct and independent principles such as freedom, equality, welfare, security, happiness etc., and that when they clash and cannot all be satisfied, we 'weigh up' the situation and finally decide that the claims of freedom, let us say, weigh heavier than those of security. Principles come to us with certain 'weights' already attached to them. Those weights, I suggest, are determined by our particular concept of man and of his essential interests. Thus the principles of the Millian liberal will be arranged roughly in a hierarchy, with self-develoment at the head. The socialist will place the principle of equality at the top of his list; and the conservative will probably allow the highest place to authority. What distinguishes the liberal from, say, the conservative is that his highest principle is individual liberty. In circumstances where he is faced with a clash betweeen the claims of liberty and those of another value (or values) the pluralistic liberal will face the problem predisposed to favour the claims of liberty. But any given situation will require to be judged on its merits, and it may be that in a given case where the claims of security, welfare, happiness or some other good are particularly strong, they will be seen even by the liberal to outweigh those of liberty.

So much in extenuation of pluralism. Mill's final position, as I have been saying earlier, remains, however, an uneasy compromise. All his

---

[5] J.P. Day, "Brian Barry, *Political Argument*", *Mind,* Vol.LXXVII (October, 1968) p.596.

days he professed to be a utilitarian; but in trying to make the principle of utility more adequate to the facts, he let into his theory elements which come into conflict with the principle of utility.

The same basic tension within the fabric of Mill's liberalism emerges again, though in a new form, in his account of the limits of liberty. He recognises the relevance and value of a variety of distinct ideals other than liberty and duly notes how they may and often do come into conflict with the ideal of liberty. In order to settle such conflicts in a rational manner, he thinks we need the guidance of a single, overall principle, which will enable us to tell what liberties are sacrosanct and what sorts of interferences with liberty are justified. If it is possible to set out and to defend such a principle, then clashes between liberty and other values may be resolved rationally and without appeal to abstract rights or to the mere preferences or feelings of the persons involved.[6] Mill is, then, attempting to formulate a general criterion which will guide the liberal in judging cases of interference with liberty. But this is to foreshadow something that can only be brought out properly by a scrutiny of Mill's views on the scope and limits of liberty, so it is to this examination I now turn.

The Reception of Mill's Principle

Beginning with the earliest reviews of Mill's famous essay, his principle of liberty has been challenged by a long line of critics and has become notorious. The principle, it is said, allows either too much or too little freedom; it is founded upon a misunderstanding of the relationship between the individual and society; when closely examined it is found, the indictment runs, to be obscure, even unintelligible. Again, it has been argued that whereas Mill purports to rest his principle on the ground of utility, his main argument for liberty turns out in fact to be not, in any standard sense, utilitarian at all.[7]

In the limited space at my disposal it is impossible I should examine these charges fully; a full treatment would, indeed, require a thesis in itself. Furthermore, there is the daunting consideration that Mill's various

---

[6] OL, p.69, pp.70-72, p.74.
[7] Karl Britton, *John Stuart Mill, op.cit.,* p.103.

formulations of his principle have lately given rise to a variety of interpretations both of its meaning and its status. In the face of this array of matters with some claim to attention, my aim will be a strictly limited one, In the remainder of this Chapter and in my final Chapter I propose to consider Mill's account of the "permanent" interests of man as it bears on the interpretation of his principle of self-protection.

My argument will be as follows. An understanding of Mill's principle of self-protection requires an understanding both of the self-regarding/other-regarding distinction and of the role of interests and rights. In terms of Mill's tripartite division of human conduct, the realm of prudence and the realm of nobility make up the area of self-regarding conduct, whilst other-regarding conduct is coextensive with the realm of the moral/immoral. Among interests, "immediate" must be distinguished from "permanent" interests, the latter being correlative with the rights dictated by 'nature' and hence with the rules of justice. In *Utilitarianism,* the rules of justice are taken to be of overwhelming importance. Consonant with this emphasis is the close link in *On Liberty* between interests and rights and the principle of self-protection. Just as Mill is concerned to demand absolute immunity from interference for *self-* regarding conduct, so he is prepared to argue conversely that an important part of other-regarding conduct, namely *unjust* other-regarding conduct, requires absolutely to be controlled.

The Sphere of Liberty

Mill's central purpose in *On Liberty* was to mark out an area in which it is possible for men and women to become self-determining so that their higher capacities might develop and flourish. He maintains:
> "there is a circle around every individual human being, which no government, be it that of one, of a few, or of the many, ought to be permitted to overstep: there is a part of the life of every person who has come to years of discretion, within which the individuality of that person ought to reign uncontrolled either by any other individual or by the public collectively. That there is, or ought to be, some space in human existence thus entrenched around, and sacred from authoritative intrusion, no one who professes the smallest regard to human freedom or dignity will call in question: the point to be determined is, where the limit should be placed;

how large a province of human life this reserved territory should include."⁸

If the individual is to be able to pursue his own good in his own way and develop his personality it is essential he be allowed an area of activity in which he is free of coercion or interference from either the state or society, an area in which he can be autonomous, can think and make decisions entirely according to his own conscience.

The problem, as Mill sees it, is how to mark out the boundary of the region within which the individual should be free from coercion by others. His general approach to this problem is thus directly in line with what we have described as his moral individualism and his conception of the essentially 'internal' nature of the good life. His view is that society and the state should uphold the 'external' or outward conditions of the life of self-development. Education and public opinion should uphold and consecrate the "social", "public", or customary morality which consittutes the general framework within which individuals and groups of individuals can work out and develop their own special forms of the good life.⁹ The central purpose of politics, the chief (though not the only) function of the state is to support and reinforce this framework by means of a system of legal sanctions. Mill's fundmental presupposition is that there are certain common conditions which must exist if all members of society are to be capable of pursuing their ideals of the good life. "All that makes existence valuable to anyone", he observes, "depends on the enforcement of restraints upon the actions of other people. Some rules of conduct, therefore, must be imposed, by law in the first place, and by opinion on many things which are not fit subjects for the operation of law."¹⁰ What these "rules laid down for general observance, under the penalties of law or opinion" ought to be is "the principal question in human affairs".

---

⁸ PPE Book V, Chapter XI, Sec.2, p.509.
⁹ See U, p.24.
¹⁰ OL, p.69.

The Principle
of Self-Protection

In the Introduction to the *Liberty* Mill observes that though most will agree about there being "a limit to the legitimate interference of collective opinion with individual independence," the "practical question, where to place the limit - how to make the fitting adjustment between individual independence and social control - is a subject on which nearly everything remains to be done."[11] The solution he offers of this problem is the famous principle of self-protection.

If Miill's principle is to be successful in enabling us to judge where to mark the boundary between what must be left to the sovereignty of the individual and what may be restrained by society then it must be given some substantial content. This is precisely what a long succession of commentators have assured us cannot possibly be done. Mill himself, it must be admitted, sent the discussion off on a wrong track in saying an agent should not be interfered with where his actions do not concern others but concern only himself. In the relevant contexts, it is conceivable Mill was misled by his own language, more especially by the ambiguous word "concerns." Certainly he has often been taken to be speaking about conduct which does not "concern" others in the sense that it is entirely private, is "self-regarding" in not having any effects on others at all. Again he speaks of "purely personal conduct"; elsewhere, of "acts and habits which are not social, but individual."[12] Since he links individuality with the enjoyment of freedom, he has been taken to be saying that a person expresses his individuality in those actions which do not affect others at all. As well as being in itself highly implausible, this view is irretrievably incompatible with Mill's selection of freedom of speech, tastes and pursuits, and association as the three main forms of activity in which men should be free. And in any case, Mill himself explicitly repudiates the view that his principle rests on a division of actions into those having or not having effects on others.[13]

---

[11] *Ibid.*, pp.68-69.
[12] *Ibid.*, p.140, p.145.
[13] See OL, pp.75, 134, 135, pp.136-38.

Interests and Rights

Not affecting, harming or injuring others can only really be taken to mean not damaging those activities of others in the enjoyment of which they are entitled to be protected. This is the line of interpretation of Mill's principle developed by J.C. Rees.[14] Rees's thesis is that an interpretation can be drawn from many (though not all) of Mill's statements in *On Liberty* which gives his principle substantial content and significant scope, which does that is to say, definitely exclude society and the state from interference with a certain sort of self-regarding conduct. On Rees's interpretation a person's conduct is self-regarding if it does not damage or endanger the interests and rights of others. Rees points out that in stating his principle Mill more than once brings in the notion of "interests" and that he fairly frequently uses the word "interests" in his explanatory and qualifying remarks. Rees observes further that Mill explains his principle also in terms of rights, sometimes linking rights with interests as, for example, in the passage where he states that self-regarding conduct "consists in not injuring the interests of one another; or rather certain interests which, either by express legal provision or by tacit understanding, ought to be considered as rights."[15] In a postscript to a recent reprint of his article Rees says he is revising his account of Mill's principle in order to give more attention to rights and to relate the principle to what is said about rights in *Utilitarianism.* [16]

My own account of the principle is like Rees's in stressing those of Mill's formulations which treat endangering or damaging the interests or rights of others as making conduct other-regarding. I qualify Rees's interpretation substantially, however, by giving a different account of interests. I shall bring to bear on Mill's references to interests and rights in the *Liberty* his analysis of the concept of a right in *Utilitarianism.* In particular I seek to illuminate Mill's conception of "permanent interests" in the *Liberty* by drawing on his view of rights as expressed in *Utilitarianism.* Through these considerations I shall be led on to a further examination of Mill's concept of morality, a topic which was opened up in my third chapter.

---

[14] In "A Re-Reading of Mill on Liberty," *op.cit.*
[15] OL, p.132. Quoted by Rees, *op.cit.*, p.122.
[16] He says, however, that he does not think this will require a substantial revision of his interpretation of Mill's principle.

On the face of it, the formulation in terms of "interests" would seem to give more scope to freedom than that in terms of not affecting others - since the latter would allow no significant freedom at all. But if Mill's principle is to be useful it must be given some content by way of a determination of the notion of "interests." If we are to be able to decide when a person's interests are endangered or damaged we must have some idea of what interests are. Rees undertakes to provide a preliminary sketch of the concept of an interest.[17] For him interests are not mere wishes, feelings, or arbitrary demands, but are things which have a more objective or stable character. Nor do interests seem to him equivalent to needs, though they may be based on needs. Rees considers but rejects the possibility that an interest is simply a claim. Rather an interest is best understood, he thinks, as the basis of a claim. An interest is involved when "a person's claim to, or title to, or share in something is recognised as valid by others, or at least is regarded as worthy of consideration."[18] This way of looking at the matter is essentially conventionalist. As Rees explains interests, they are not present unless a claim either is recognised as socially valid or is generally thought of as a worthy candidate for such recognition. Interests "depend for their existence on social recognition, and are closely connected with prevailing standards about the sort of behaviour a man can legitimately expect from others."[19] Yet when Rees moves on from a discussion of the concept of an interest to a consideration of what things are to count as interests he acknowledges that since "standards and values enter into what will be recognised as interests" there will be certain things which some groups recognise as interests which will not be recognised as such by society generally.[20] He thinks that while there are situations in which it is relatively easy to discover what are generally conceded to be interests, e.g. in the case of "legal interests", there are other situations where, because values differ, people will disagree as to what their interests are.

---

[17] Rees, *op.cit.*, pp.118-19, 124-27.
[18] *Ibid.*, p.125.
[19] *Ibid.*, p.119. Or as he puts it on a later page (125) "interests are things we would generally look upon as deserving protection."
[20] *Ibid.*, p.126.

It seems to me that broadly speaking there are three categories of interests. Clearly, there is a large number of determinate (socially recognised) interests upheld by legal rights; then there are other interests which though not supported by legal sanctions, are commonly looked upon as morally deserving of protection; and, thirdly, there are some things claimed by some to be interests but not generally thought to be such. In Rees's version, it seems Mill's principle is to be understood to refer to conduct not injuring interests that fall into the first two categories. This interpretation of Rees is called for by his own conventionalist definition of "interests" together with his claim that there is nothing in *On Liberty* to suggest Mill did not adhere to a conventionalist notion of interests.

We could then understand Rees's version of Mill's principle as stating that the question of whether a person's freedom should be restricted could not be raised unless his conduct affected prejudicially these socially recognised interests. Now, this would certainly give the principle determinate content and scope such as to allow (in many societies) considerable though bounded freedom. There clearly are many actions which affect others without affecting their socially constituted interests. And there are some lines of conduct which may even be said to harm others without damaging their interests. An example would be Mill's case of those who succeed in an overcrowded profession.

Rees's version of Mill's principle is nevertheless open to a serious objection. Because of his conventionalist definition of interests as what are actually established legally or socially within a given society, Rees imports into Mill's principle a decidedly conservative bias. But Mill himself thinks of his principle as innovatory;[21] he takes himself to be opposing a social morality which had made what he thought of as illegitimate claims concerning interests and rights. Rees's version has the limits of appropriate social and legal interference set by what, in a given society, are as a matter of fact established as interests. But it is clear that this version cannot be reconciled with a doctrine Mill designed expressly to provide a

---

[21] Cf. Ted Honderich, "Mill on Liberty", *Inquiry*, Vol.10 (1967) pp.292-97. Honderich argues that, for Mill, recognised or established interests are valid only if they accord with utility; but he does not (as I shall do) connect utility with man's permanent interests.

criterion which would test whether interferences socially established as proper and justified by recognised 'interests' are indeed justified.

If Mill's principle were to be based on socially established interests it might not allow some of the liberties he is most anxious to defend, and the area of freedom mapped by the principle might well be reduced very greatly. In order to reinforce this claim I draw attention to Mill's own expressions of attitude towards his principle. He says that though his doctrine is anything but new and may even for some have "the air of a truism" there is nevertheless "no doctrine which stands more directly opposed to the general tendency of existing opinion and practice".[22] In general, what Mill is objecting to is that the "likings and dislikings of society" are, in practice, the main thing which has "determined the rules laid down for general observance, under the penalties of law or opinion".[23] He sees himself as being in advance of the social opinion of his own day in regarding certain prevailing standards about what conduct it is appropriate for men to expect from others as being illegitimate. He wants to use his principle of self-protection to establish certain "rights of the individual against society",[24] a society which "has expended fully as much effort in the attempt (according to its lights) to compel people to conform to its notions of personal as of social excellence".[25] These rights, as I shall presently argue, are grounded on social utility understood as embracing certain "permanent" or fundamental interests of man.

That Mill did not intend his principle to be based simply on interests sanctioned by social recognition is again implied by a formulation of the principle near the beginning of Chapter IV of the *Liberty*. He there maintains that each person ought to adopt a certain line of conduct which "consists, first, in not injuring the interests of one another; or rather certain interests, which, either by express legal provision or tacit understanding, *ought* to be considered as rights."[26] There are, we may take Mill to be claiming, certain interests which because of their special importance should be considered as rights. The rights Mill is most concerned to protect

---
[22] OL, p.76.
[23] *Ibid.*, p.70.
[24] *Ibid.*, p.71.
[25] *Ibid.*, p.76.
[26] OL, p.132. My italics.

are the very ones deriving from this special class of interests (a class whose criterion of membership is independent of social recognition).

Mill's Doctrine of Interests

In this Introduction to *On Liberty,* Mill explicitly repudiates any appeal to "the idea of abstract right, as a thing independent of utility". In the very next sentence, however, he invokes, as "the ultimate appeal on all ethical questions," a conception of "utility in the largest sense, grounded on the permanent interests of man as a progressive being."[27] R.F. Anschutz has complained that Mill nowhere elaborates a positive theory of these "permanent interests".[28] But if my account of Mill's conception of man has been on the right lines then Anschutz's complaint is seriously misleading. While Mill does not explicitly articulate a conception of man, he does indeed, as we saw, rely heavily upon a certain conception of man. And as I shall argue, this model or conception of man - of what man is at his best or what he has it in him to become - involves a specific theory as to which of men's intersts are the most important or essential.

Now since the notion of an interest is by no means clear and unambiguous, it will be helpful, as a preliminary to discussing which among men's interests Mill takes to be the most vital, to give some attention to how, in general, he understands the notion of an interest.

Bentham operated entirely with a psychological concept of 'interests': action, he maintained, is in a man's interests if it "tends to add to the sum of his pleasures". He understood the individual's interests, then, to be the satisfaction of his immediate wants. In general, Mill too adheres to such a psychological or naturalistic use of 'interests', in which interests are linked with people's present wants or desires, with what they are currently interested in or concerned with, psychologically speaking. For him, 'X is in A's interest' is equivalent to saying X is what would satisfy A's immediate wants or desires. The sense of 'interests' involved is that used by Mill in *Utilitarianism* when he says that happiness may "practically speaking" be

---
[27] OL, p.74.
[28] R.F. Anschutz, *op.cit.,* p.24.

called the interest of an individual.[29] To be caused pain or loss is, for Mill, the paradigm of damage to one's interests.[30] To say, then, that conduct damages the interests of others is, in this very general sense of 'interests', equivalent to saying that it "harms" them, causes them "evil"; it is to say that it is "hurtful to others", is "injurious" to them, or causes them "perceptible hurt".[31]

In "Coleridge" Mill takes Bentham to task for failing to analyse the concept of "interest". He points out that when we speak of a man's 'interest' we may sometimes have in mind something that Bentham himself overlooked; we may mean "what would appear such to a calculating bystander, judging what would be good for a man during his whole life, and making no account or but little, of the gratification of his present passions".[32] Mill makes the very same distinction in *Representative Government*. He says that when we talk of the interest of a man or group of men we may mean "what would be considered their interest by an unprejudiced observer" or we may mean what is "practically a man's interest" - his "immediate and direct" (often selfish) interest.[33] Mill's point may be glossed as that simply to say something is in a person's interest is ambiguous: it could mean that it will satisfy his immediate wants; it could mean that it is for his ultimate interest, objectively conceived; or it could mean both of these things.

The normative approach to interests here adumbrated by Mill accords with recent and fuller explications of the concept by Stanley Benn and R.S. Peters.[34] Following their accounts we may say that in speaking of someone's interest we ordinarily have in mind something which is important to him or for which he has a *concern*. Interests are what is or

---

[29] U, p.16.
[30] OL, p.150; PPE, p.569.
[31] OL, pp.73, 74, 135, 138.
[32] "Coleridge" in Himmelfarb, *op.cit.,* p.161. And compare also this passage: "The heartiness of Mr. Thornton's devotion to the interest of the labouring classes (or, it should rather be said, to the interest of human nature as embodied in them) is manifested throughout the work."
"Thornton on Labour and its Claims",, *Collected Works,* Vol.5, p.658.
[33] RG, pp.251-52.
[34] S.I. Benn, "'Interests' in Politics" in *Proceedings of the Aristotelian Society,* Vol.LX, 1959-60. R.S. Peters, *Ethics and Education, op.cit.,* pp.167-70.

ought to be of concern to persons. We can then go on to distinguish between a psychological[35] and a normative use of "interests', between, in Benn's terminology, a "naturalistic" and a "normative" use. In the psychological or naturalistic sense, interests are linked with people's wants or desires, to what they are interested in or concerned with psychologically speaking. Brian Barry has recently offered an analysis of the concept of interests along psychological lines. A definition he considers only to reject is the following: " 'X is in A's interest' [is] equivalent to 'A wants X' ".[36] The ground for the rejection is that this definition rules out our asking " 'A wants X but is it in his interests?' "[37] Even so, his final account remains an instrumental, want-regarding account of interests: "To say... that an action or policy is in somebody's interests is not actually to say that it satisfies his immediate wants at all; it is rather to say it puts him in a better position to satisfy his wants."[38] In short, he rejects the normative or (in his own terms) "ideal-regarding" view of interests suggested by Mill and elaborated by Benn and Peters.

A fuller consideration of the issues raised by these recent analyses of interests is outside the scope of my thesis. I should agree with Peters, though, that it seems perfectly possible for someone to act in another's interests without necessarily paying attention either to his immediate wants or to what will increase his opportunities to satisfy foreseeable future wants. "For... though we think it regrettable that some people cannot get what they want, we also think it regrettable that other people want just what they get. In other words judgments are passed on people's wants in deciding what is in their interest."[39] There is, it would seem, a well established normative notion of 'interests' according to which we judge whether some action or policy is in a person's interests in terms of whether or not it measures up to some standard or norm. Thus when the teacher acts in the interests of a schoolchild he may be concerned not so much with enhancing the child's opportunities for satisfying certain wants as with educating him to be a human being of a certain sort. (Benn invokes this traditional example.) It is extremely doubtful whether Barry's contrast

---

[35] See R.S. Peters, *Ethics and Education*, *ibid.*, p.167.
[36] Brian Barry, *op.cit.*, p.175.
[37] *Ibid.*, p.175.
[38] *Ibid.*, p.183.
[39] R.S. Peters, *op.cit.*, p.170.

between "want-satisfaction now and want-satisfaction later"[40] is a rich enough model to do justice to the distinction we commonly make in such a case. For the notion of *want-satisfaction later* still treats a man's wants as a class of items of data, whereas just what is in question is a notion of a man's interest which is invoked in justification of our acting to modify the kind of wants he may come to have. This is the kind of consideration we have in mind in saying the situation may be that what a person wants either now or in the future may not be in his 'objective' interests. By this I mean what Mill meant, namely that what a person's interests are may depend not just on what wants he seeks to gratify but as well on an independent evaluation of what is the best and happiest life. If this is so, then, as against Barry, some judgments of what is in a person's interests necessarily do involve "ideal-regarding" principles, are related to what is thought to be a worthwhile form of life.

According to Mill, we say that a policy or an action is in a man's "ultimate" or "permanent" interest when looking at it disinterestedly we judge it would be good for him "during his whole life". Such judgments as to what is in a person's permanent interest may, then, be said to presuppose some ideal of what it is good for a man to be. Further, in speaking of the permanent interests of man Mill has it in mind that there are certain fundmental interests a man has on account of his human nature. Some judgments concerning what is in a person's "ultimate" interests are not relative to any specific individual; for there are some very general conditions or 'needs' which any person must satisfy if he is to develop his potentialities. These interests may be said to be especially crucial for well-being in the case of each and every individual.

Mill on Interests and Rights

More light may be cast on Mill's interpretation of the notion of such a permanent interest by way of his view of rights as set out in *Utilitarianism.* Mill took himself to be discarding the seventeenth and eighteenth century doctrine of natural rights. While remaining firmly attached to the particular

---

[40] Brian Barry, *op.cit.,* p.185.

rights claimed by the natural rights theorists, he sought in the notion of utility a firmer, less metaphysical foundation on which to ground them. What he tried to do is to show that the much greater weight we allow to certain individual rights can be explained on strictly Utilitarian grounds. Yet, as we shall presently see, in fact he introduces qualifications into his conception of utility which strongly suggest that he is really importing into it the notion of a natural right, that he smuggles in natural rights under the guise of special utilities.

Mill's primary aim in Chapter V of *Utilitarianism* is to defend the view that justice is a "branch" or species of general utility. Prior to examining the relationship between the two concepts he undertakes a clarification of the notion of justice. He sets down five "modes of action, and arrangements of human affairs"[41] that are commonly classed as just or unjust and then asks what each of his five examples of just conduct has in common. He finds two common features: (1) If a line of conduct is just then any person who deliberately avoids such conduct may properly receive punishment for so doing; (2) If a line of conduct is just, then some specific person or group has a *right* to demand that that conduct be performed. Proposition (1) marks off "morality in general, from the remaining provinces of expediency and worhiness."[42] Even though it is the case that anyone who is unjust deserves punishment,[43] it is also true that some who are deserving of punishment could not be called unjust, but only, say, lacking in generosity. Proposition (2) carries Mill's account a step further, and "distinguishes justice from other branches of morality."[44] The region of justice is that in which there are duties with correlative rights. "Justice implies something which it is not only right to do, and wrong not to do, but which some individual person can claim from us as his moral right."[45]

---

[41] U, p.40.
[42] *Ibid.*, p.46. Compare my previous discussion in Chapter III.
[43] Punishment is understood in a broad sense, so as to include not only the operation of the more direct sanctions but such things as the pains of suffering disapprobation, the pangs of conscience.
[44] U, p.46.
[45] *Ibid.*, p.46. In addition to the demand for punishment, justice involves "the conception of some definite person who suffers by the infringement; whose rights. . . are violated by it". (*Ibid.*, p.49.)

Mill's account so far may be related to his general breakdown of human conduct discussed earlier in the thesis and especially in Chapter III and the whole scheme presented as in the **diagram** on page 164.

A little later in his discussion Mill raises the question of what we mean by ascribing a right to a certain person. His answer is that if "we call anything a person's right, we mean that he has a valid claim on society to protect him in the possession of it, either by the force of law, or by that of education and opinion."[46] Thus if and only if we think there should be some legal or moral rule prohibiting interference with a person's use of certain things, his engaging in certain activities, his development of specific capacities and so forth, are we willing to grant him any right to make use of such things, carry out such actions etc. So the statement that a person has a right to something is, in Mill's view, equivalent to the statement that there exists an obligation to create and maintain a rule or institution which will help him to gain and keep possession of the thing in question.

If we now ask how it is possible to demonstrate the existence of such an obligation then the only answer Mill thinks it possible to give is "general utility;" i.e. the ultimate foundation or ground of all rights is general utility. But in this context he adds that it is an "extraordinarily important and impressive kind of utility which is concerned."[47] From the viewpoint of Mill's conception of the permanent interests of man, the significance of this answer lies in its close correspondence to the way in which he qualifies the principle of utility in the Introduction to *On Liberty*. The account of rights Mill now goes on to present is indispensable to an understanding of the conception of permanent interests he sketches in the *Liberty*. In *Utilitarianism,* then, Mill writes:

> "To have a right, then is, I conceive, to have something which society ought to defend me in the possession of. If the objector goes on to ask, why it ought? I can give him no other reason than general utility. . . The interest involved is that of security, to everyone's feelings the most vital of all interests. . . security no human being can possibly do without; on it we depend for all our immunity from evil, and for the whole value of all and every good, beyond the passing moment; since nothing but the gratification of the instant could be of any worth to us, if we could be deprived of anything the next instant by whoever was momentarily

---
[46] *Ibid.,* p.49.
[47] *Ibid.,* p.50.

HUMAN CONDUCT

1. MORALITY:
The area of *moral obligations*, which entail duty to fulfil, the meriting of punishment for failure to fulfil. Punishment in the range direct sanctions to pains of disapprobation, conscience pangs.

1a. JUSTICE:
The area of duty to protect the permanent interests of others, i.e. to say to protect the (moral, perhaps legal) fundamental rights of assignable persons, such as the right to equal freedom.

1a₁. The area of duty *not to injure* the interests of assignable persons.
Examples: duty to refrain from theft, assault.

1a₂. The area of duty to act *positively to protect* the permanent interests of others.
Example: duty to restrain and warn man about to step on unsound bridge.

1b. WIDER MORAL OBLIGATION:
The area of what it is our duty to do, yet as contrasted with 1a if we fail to fulfil we do not breach a right of any assignable person.
Examples from area 1b: generosity, beneficence.

2. EXPEDIENCY (PRUDENCE):
The area of instrumentally efficient / inefficient behaviour.

3. WORTHINESS:
The area of commendable / unworthy activities of the noble and the aesthetic.
Example from area 3: Self-development or its neglect

> stronger than ourselves. Now this most indispensable of all necessaries, after physical nutriment, cannot be had, unless the machinery for providing it is kept unintermittently in active play. Our notion, therefore, of the claim we have on our fellow creatures to join in making safe for us the very groundwork of our existence, gathers feelings around it so much more intense than those concerned in any of the more common cases of utility, that the difference in degree. . . becomes a real difference in kind."[48]

Mill is here laying it down that security is something none of us can do without. But what, more precisely, makes security a "vital interest", thus ultimately establishing, in the only possible way, that every human being has a right to it? Mill, as I understand him, is advancing the traditional Hobbesian view according to which security is constantly endangered by conduct tending towards a state of nature. Mill holds that security is the most vital of all man's interests since without it we could scarcely continue in existence, let alone continue to do the things we think worth doing. It is of such central concern that no man could live, or at any rate develop as a human being, in its absence.

If this interpretation of Mill is allowed, permanent interests may be said to be associated with certain central human needs such as, for example, the need for security. In the light of this account we may summarise Mill's view of the way to ground claims about the possession of rights as follows. The only compelling evidence it is possible to bring forward in support of claims to rights consists in propositions showing them to be related to certain permanent interests. There are enduring central interests, certain conditions or states of affairs which are or ought to be the concern of all normal human beings; and these interests are the ultimate grounds of our rights. Thus, the interest in security of person and property is of concern to all men simply as men, i.e. as distinct from their specific interests as members of some particular community, or as persons of some particular character. What, for Mill, distinguishes rules of justice from other moral rules (so that they involve essentially the protection afforded by a right) is their indispensable function in protecting our well-being.
> "Justice", as he says, "is a name for certain classes of moral rules, which concern the essentials of human well-being more nearly, and are therefore of more absolute obligation, than any other rules for the guidance of life; and the notion which we have found to be the essence of the idea of justice,

---
[48] *Ibid.,* p.50.

that of a right residing in an individual, implies and testifies to this more binding obligation".[49]

He then goes on to single out the right to equal freedom as among the rights which society has an obligation to provide and each individual has a right to demand. This principle of our right to equal freedom and obligation to uphold equal freedom is much more basic than the principle of our obligation to be positively beneficent. (Here there is no corresponding right of claim by specifiable individuals). The reason is that while an individual may possibly not need benefits from others he *always* has a "need" not to have his freedom wrongfully curtailed:

> "The moral rules which forbid mankind to hurt one another (in which we must never forget to include wrongful interference with each other's freedom) are more vital to human well-being than any maxims, however important, which only point out the best mode of managing some department of human affairs. . . Thus the moralities which protect every individual from being harmed by others, either directly or by being hindered in his freedom of pursuing his own good, are at once those which he himself has most at heart, and those which he has the strongest interest in publishing and enforcing by word and deed. . . Now it is these moralities primarily which compose the obligations of justice."[50]

Since every man has a need not to be hindered in pursuing his own good he may accordingly be said to have the "strongest interest" in seeing freedom maintained. Non-interference is thus, for Mill, one of the obligations to which we are bound in justice, one of the "social utilities which are vastly more important, and therefore more absolute and imperative, than any others are as a class."[51]

It is an analytic matter for Mill that justice is a mode of utility. Written into the principle of utility are certain fundamental moral rules or rights, including those of non-interference, impartiality, equality, veracity. Distinguished from other moral rules by their being "more vital to human well-being", these are thus the fundamental precepts of justice.

---

[49] *Ibid.*, p.55.
[50] *Ibid.*, pp.55-56.
[51] *Ibid.*, p.55.

In summary, then, the position is as follows. Where a moral rule is just there exists a right of specifiable individuals to have the rule obeyed and to have conformity to it guaranteed by institutions. "Social utilities" of a "vastly important" kind are the ground of our funadmental rights. Utility in this "extraordinarily important and impressive" sense concerns "the essentials of human well-being". In these essentials every individual man has the deepest of interests. These are his "vital" interests, foundation of his most fundmental rights.

The account of vital interests and their associated rights in *Utilitarianism* is correlative to Mill's distinction elsewhere between "immediate" and "ultimate" (or "permanent") interests. Again vital interests are associated with ultimate needs - though neither the interests nor the needs are of necessity accorded social recognition, nor even consciously recognised by their individual possessor. Simply from his distinctively human nature, an individual has a *prima facie* right not to be interefered with, a right to be treated impartially and so on. Again there are invoked the fundamental interests that are of overriding concern to human individuals, interests (and associated rights) which it behoves us to give priority, generally speaking, over all others.

CHAPTER XI

THE PRINCIPLE OF SELF-PROTECTION

Utility and Permanent Interests.

The above interpretation of Mill's account of rights and interests can be seen to illuminate Mill's defence of liberty in *On Liberty*. This new light makes it clear that Mill's avowal of the ultimate grounds of his vindication of liberty cannot be dismissed as a mere empty gesture towards pious Benthamite sentiment. It has frequently been taken to be the case that the substance of Mill's arguments for liberty does not really rest on an appeal to utility, notwithstanding that he pays lipservice to the idea of utilitarian justification. I have opened the way to showing that, on the contrary, he does indeed hold utility to be the final principle of morality. But, to repeat, "it must be utility in the largest sense, grounded on the permanent interests of a man as a progressive being."[1] Mill is hereby giving his readers fair warning that while he intends to defend liberty on the ground of its utility, the sense of 'utility' he has in mind is very different from that associated with a hedonistic, Benthamite liberalism. He does defend liberty (i.e. non-interference) in terms of the greatest happiness principle, but it is in terms of the principle expanded in such a way as to include what he regards as the most essential ingredients in human happiness (though a Benthamite would not have agreed with him). Thus most of his arguments do not relate to liberty as a means to happiness where 'happiness' is understood simply as a favourable balance of pleasure over pain. Instead, he argues for non-interference as a condition of individuality, self-development, knowledge, rational belief and morally responsible conduct. On the other hand, he simply takes it for granted that constraint is always painful, or at least irksome, so that this is an assumption lying behind all his arguments in favour of non-interference.

Consider first Mill's well-known arguments for freedom of speech. For these four particular arguments bring out very well that lying behind

---

[1] OL, p.74.

specific arguments for freedom is his conception of man's "permanent interests as a progressive being." The four particular arguments - the censor assumes his own infallibility, etc. are brought to show that freedom of speech is a means of promoting diversity of opinion, truth, lively belief, mental development, moral improvement and intellectual and moral progress. The promotion and protection of these goods will, Mill thinks, contribute greatly to the self-development and happiness of mankind. The purpose of the whole of Chapter II is summarised by him in conclusion as to show the usefulness of freedom of speech in promoting "the mental well-being of mankind (on which all their other well-being depends)."[2] His arguments, he believes, show that unless men are free to form and express their opinions there will be "baneful consequences to the intellectual, and through that to the moral nature of man."[3] That is to say, in Mill's own terms, men will be deprived of happiness.

It might seem (and has seemed to some) that while in the vindication of individuality in Chapter III considerations of permanent interests and of human well-being are in the forefront of Mill's discussion, in the vindication of free speech in Chapter II these considerations have by contrast only a shadowy part to play. It is true that considerations of permanent interests and human well-being is relegated to the background in Chapter II. The reason is that Mill would have felt their application to what he dwells on at length is relatively uncontroversial. It would be agreed, he would have assumed, that truth, mental development and moral improvement, say, i.e. things he does show in detail to be promoted by free speech, are in turn contributory to human well-being. But individuality Mill takes to be a neglected interest. Hence in Chapter III he feels the need to make plain at every step the permanent interest men have in nurturing individuality and the vital contribution it makes to their well-being.

Mill's appeal to the concept of a permanent interest in the vindication of individuality is, then, especially overt for polemical reasons. To some extent it is generally admitted, Mill feels, that we should have our own opinions, but there is not the same willingness to admit that our desires and impulses should be our own and that they are as much a part of "a perfect

---

[2] *Ibid.*, p.111.
[3] *Ibid.*, p.114.

human being" as are our homegrown beliefs.[4] Mill thought that in his own day individuality was one of "the neglected interests", a "side of human well-being"[5] scarcely recognised by common opinion (or even by most moral and social reformers) as "having any intrinsic worth, or deserving any regard on its own account."[6] There had been a period when spontaneity or individuality was so strong as to threaten the fabric of society. But in modern times the general tendency has been for collective, mediocre opinion to get the upper hand and the upshot is that the "danger which threatens human nature is not the excess, but the deficiency of personal impulses and preferences."[7] Hence, in order to counteract and correct this tendency there is a special need to emphasize strongly the value of individuality, and particularly the individuality of the gifted and cultivated few.[8] Unless we do this, mankind will not continue to improve (Europe may even become another China) and man will cease to be a progressive being.[9]

The reliance on the notion of man's permanent interests in Mill's defence of individuality has been explored at length in my Chapters IV and V. Here I have simply drawn attention to the way this reliance links up with Mill's overall reliance on his extended conception of utility (utility grounded on man's permanent interests) and thus with the basic architectonic of his defence of liberty.

Permanent Interests, Rights and Self-Protection

Mill's liberty-limiting principle depends on the distinction between self-regarding and other-regarding conduct. In the sphere of other-regarding conduct the notion of what it is to affect the permanent interests of others, hence their rights, has a special place. This final section of my thesis is devoted to considering the self-regarding/other-regarding

---

[4] *Ibid.,* pp.117-18.
[5] *Ibid.,* p.107.
[6] *Ibid.,* p.115.
[7] *Ibid.,* p.119.
[8] *Ibid.,* p.124.
[9] *Ibid.,* pp.127-29.

distinction in such a way as to locate the special place occupied by permanent interests and rights.

The permanent interests of man are in securing those fundamental conditions which any and every man needs if he is to live a good or even a tolerable life. A man may have certain interests which are peculiar to himself, but he will have other basic interests in common with every other man. Mill is everywhere keen to stress that among this latter group comprising the most vital of interests, common to all, must be included man's interest in securing the right to equal freedom.[10]

Man's permanent interests, Mill says, "authorise the subjection of individual spontaneity to external control, only in respect of those actions of each, which concern the interests of other people"[11] This dictum raises once again the question of how Mill's liberty-limiting principle is to be interpreted. By "interests" in this passage Rees understands Mill to mean those interests which are established, or socially recognised, in a given society. Thus self-regarding actions would be those actions which concern only the interest of the agent himself; actions would be taken out of the self-regarding category and become other-regarding when they endanger or damage the (socially recognised) interests of others.

Several other recent writers have interpreted Mill's principle differently from Rees. Alan Ryan, for instance, draws upon Mill's threefold division of human conduct into the moral, the prudential and the aesthetic/noble to argue that self-regarding actions are restricted to the prudential and aesthetic spheres whereas other-regarding actions are coextensive with moral actions.[12] This view is very similar to that adopted by A.R. Louch in an article "Sins and Crimes".[13] Traditionally it has been assumed that Mill is trying to isolate from interference an area of private, moral (or immoral) conduct. Louch argues that self-regarding activities fall into the area of the non-moral. For Louch, as for Ryan, Mill makes no intrinsic distinction between law and morality; a distinction is taken to be

---
[10] Outside the *Liberty,* see especially U, pp.55-56 and cf., e.g. *Autobiography, op.cit.,* p.179.
[11] OL, p.74.
[12] Ryan, *loc.cit.*
[13] Louch, *loc.cit.* See also M. Singer, *loc.cit.*

made, but its basis is extrinsic - law is distinguished from morality according to the kind of sanctions it is backed with, direct sanctions as distinct from the sanctions of public or social opinion which are used to back morality. For Ryan and Louch, Mill's main concern is to prevent interference (by either legal or social sanctions) in conduct which is not moral at all. The main distinction Mill wishes to draw is taken to be one between *self-* regarding activities, which are private or concern only the agent himself and in which morality is not involved, and *other-* regarding activities which do involve morality and for which legal and/or social sanctions may appropriately be invoked. According to this view, Mill's principle may be understood as confining morality to the other-regarding realm.

An interpretation of Mill's principle resembling that just outlined has been put forward by Gabriele Taylor and Sybil Wolfram.[14] Put very roughly, their contention is that Mill's distinction is between conduct that, largely speaking, benefits/harms only the agent himself and conduct which benefits/harms others. The Taylor-Wolfram interpretation, though, differs from that of Ryan and Louch in not eliminating self-regarding conduct from the realm of the moral. Taylor and Wolfram speak of Mill's distinction as one between the self-regarding and the other-regarding "virtues". This, though is an error. According to Mill, virtuous conduct is necessarily concerned with the (disinterested) promotion of the good of others. For him the self-regarding "qualities" (as he usually calls them) are not properly virtues nor are the self-regarding "failings" strictly speaking vices - though it is true he occasionally lapses into the language of morality and speaks of self-regarding "virtues".

A serious inadequacy common to the Ryan, Louch and Taylor-Wolfram interpretations of Mill's account of other-regarding action is, as it seems to me, their failure to take account of his frequent use of the notions of rights and interests. Rees's account of other-regarding actions has, indeed, a comparable blemish, for though he duly emphasises the notions of interests and rights, his interpretation suffers both from a mistaken view of

---

[14] "Mill, Punishment and the Self-Regarding Failings," *Analysis,* Vol.28, No.5 (April,1968) and "The Self-Regarding and Other-Regarding Virtues", *The Philsophical Quarterly,* Vo.18, No72 (July, 1968). Both articles are jointly written.

the use Mill makes of rights and interests in relation to the liberty-limiting principle and (at least to some extent) from a misconception of Mill's notion of rights and interests. On the side of self-regarding conduct Rees's account is, moreover, incomplete in the area where Ryan, Louch and Taylor and Wolfram are - in varying degrees - more adequate. All these latter writers give a somewhat fuller positive characterization of self-regarding conduct as Mill understood it. (The incompleteness is to some extent justifiable in Rees, since his concern is primarily with the other-regarding side of the principle; the criteria for discriminating the two sides are interdependent, however, and it is of the essence to characterize the contrast adequately.)

The Self-Regarding Excluded from Morality

Now the kinds of conduct (and of dispositions) Mill takes to be self-regarding are those kinds which do not necessarily or from their nature (i.e. according to the way we define that sort of conduct) affect (adversely or otherwise) the interest or well-being of anyone but the agent himself. There is this important qualification: where the interest of another is necessarily affected, but only with his free and undeceived consent, the conduct remains within the self-regarding sphere (fornication between consenting partners is an example). It should be stressed that the way in which the self-regarding has just been characterised relates to universals of conduct (and of dispositions which may be manifested in conduct). Thus if we say that extravagance, drunkenness or reading poetry are self-regarding, we must remember, in relating this claim to the conduct of some particular man, that it is only its extravagant, drunken, or poetry-reading aspects that are touched by the claim. Some particular spending spree, bender, or week of poetry-reading indulged in by Bloggs might also constitute neglect of his family or other obligations. The claim has nothing to say about this aspect of Bloggs's conduct. His very same conduct will in its neglect-of-responsibilities aspect be other-regarding:

> "If. . . a man, through intemperance or extravagance becomes unable to pay his debts, or, having undertaken the moral responsibility of a family, becomes from the same cause incapable of supporting or educating them, he is deservedly reprobated, and might be justly punished; but it

is for the breach of duty to his famiy or creditors, not for the extravagance."[15]

Seen in relation to Mill's three-fold division of human conduct (into the spheres of morality; expediency; excellence or worthiness), self-regarding conduct embraces both the sphere of the prudent and that of the excellent (noble/aesthetic), i.e. it is, strictly speaking, non-moral. As he explains in *Utilitarianism,* there are things:

> ". . . which we wish that people should do, which we like or admire them for doing, perhaps dislike or despise them for not doing, but yet admit that they are not bound to do; it is not a case of moral obligation; we do not blame them, that is, we do not think that they are proper objects of punishment. . .we say it would be right to do so and so, or merely that it would be desirable or laudable, according as we would wish to see the person whom it concerns, compelled, or only persuaded or exhorted, to act in that manner."[16]

In terms of Mill's central purpose of giving "to duty on the one hand and to freedom and spontaneity on the other their proper province,"[17] the self-regarding department of human affairs is the "appropriate region" of liberty, alternatively the "province of liberty", in which "individual spontaneity is entitled to free exercise."[18] Questions relating to self-regarding conduct are "essentially questions of liberty."[19] For Mill, liberty as meaning non-interference is essentially the absence of obligation, i.e. the absence of a moral rule backed by the sanction of either legal or social punishment. Self-regarding qualities (or failings) are not proper subjects for the employment of punishment or compulsion; it is by education or persuasion only that self-regarding conduct may be controlled.[20] Conduct within the self-regarding area may be evidence of "any amount of folly, or want of personal dignity and self-respect;" but such actions are "only a subject of moral reprobation when they involve a breach of duty to others."[21]

---

[15] OL, p.138.
[16] U, p.45.
[17] "Utility of Religion", *op.cit.,* p.71.
[18] OL, p.75, p.133, p.138.
[19] *Ibid.,* p.151.
[20] *Ibid.,* p.133.
[21] *Ibid.,* p.135.

Mill is asking for the toleration of self-regarding conduct. Neither society nor the state has any business to interfere with the self-regarding aspect of a person's conduct. Society "has no business, *as* society, to decide anything to be wrong which concerns only the individual."[22] What he is especially concerned to prevent is interference with persons for their own good. He wants individual freedom to be secure against those who "have occupied themselves rather in arguing what things society ought to like or dislike, than in questioning whether its likings or dislikings should be a law to individuals."[23] There was a strong tendency, Mill thought, for the public to turn every question of conduct into a moral one, to call 'moral' what was properly the concern only of the individual, in an attempt to extenuate unwarranted interference. There was a strong tendency to extend the authority of "moral police" so as to impose on everyone people's preferences, tastes, feelings, irritations, revulsions and so on, and so to give these non-moral attitudes the status of moral laws. Such attitudes were, for instance, exemplified by those strict Calvinists and Methodists who wished to prohibit or severely restrict such amusements or recreations as music, dancing, and the theatre; and were enshrined in Sabbatarian legislation. Illiberal attitudes are strongly reinforced by the Intuitionist strain in "nine-tenths of all moralists and speculative writers" who "teach that things are right because they are right; because we feel them to be so."[24] Mill would put the onus on such people to show that the activities they complain of are *morally* wrong - something they could only do, he claimed, by showing that the activities do as a matter of fact harm or damage the interests of other people.

The fact that the self-regarding qualities are not subject to moral evaluation, to praise or blame or to punishment does not mean that they are unimportant.[25] The self-regarding qualities are "only second in importance, if even second, to the social" and it is the business of education

---

[22] *Ibid.*, p.154 (italics in original); cf. pp.68, 142, 143.
[23] *Ibid.*, pp.70-71.
[24] *Ibid.*, p.141.
[25] Contrast Taylor and Wolfram who lump Mill together with writers they claim take the self-regarding "virtues" as those which will benefit largely the agent himself and so suggest that "to develop the self-regarding virtues is much less important and wholly self-interested." "The Self-Regarding and Other-Regarding Virtues," *op.cit.*, pp.238-39. Certain other moral writers may indeed have thought what Taylor and Wolfram attribute to Mill - Mill assuredly did not.

to develop them.26 We should be forever employing conviction and persuasion in order to stimulate others to "increased exercise of their higher faculties, and increased direction of their feelings and aims towards wise instead of foolish, elevating instead of degrading, objects and contemplations."27 Furthermore, the person who possesses the self-regarding qualities in a high degree is "so much nearer to the ideal of human nature" and entirely worthy of our admiration and emulation. On the other hand, the person who manifests to a degree the self-regarding deficiencies - who shows extreme foolishness, say, or exhibits low and depraved taste - is quite properly an object of dislike or, in extreme cases, an object of contempt.

The Other-Regarding Coextensive with Moral Conduct

Other-regarding conduct is that which essentially concerns the interests of other persons. By 'interests' in general Mill means (as we saw) simply "well-being" or "happiness". To say, then, that conduct damages the interests of others is in this very general sense of 'interests' equivalent to saying it causes them harm or injury.

Since other-regarding conduct is that which essentially affects the interests or welfare of others, it is coextensive with moral conduct. This is the realm in which we have duties or obligations and may legitimately be punished for failing to fulfil them. To say that an action is *im* moral is, in Mill's view, to way that it will endanger or damage the interests of persons other than the agent. Mill's principle amounts to a limitation of morality to conduct that effects others without their free and undeceived consent. As Ryan puts it, "it is only to this sort of conduct that appraisal in terms of *wrong, immoral,* or *wicked* is appropriate. And, crucially, it is only in the area of this sort of conduct that deterrence and retribution as they operate in morals - that is, social approval and disapproval, the weapons of public opinion - can ever be justified."28 As soon as conduct affects prejudicially the interests of others it becomes immoral and so, in principle, subject to

---

26 OL, p.133.
27 *Ibid.*
28 Ryan, *The Listener, op.cit.,* p.621. Italics in original.

legal or social control. If it can be shown that conduct endangers or damages the interests or well-being of others, a *prima facie* case has been made out for invoking against the agent either legal or social sanctions.[29]

Ryan correctly argues that the distinction upon which Mill wished to insist "is not a distinction between law and morality, but between the sort of conduct subject to law-or-morality on the one hand and that which is subject to neither of these but to prudential or aesthetic appraisal on the other."[30] In making other-regarding conduct coextensive with the area of the moral Ryan is so far correct. But Ryan does not make any explicit reference to interests or rights in his version of Mill's account of other-regarding conduct (and nor, as I have said, does Louch), whereas both notions play a conspicuous role in Mill's account.

Justice and Other-Regarding Conduct

In general, Mill employs "interests" in the very wide sense in which it is equivalent to "well-being". Where it is only in this very wide sense that interests enter Mill's account there is no problem presented for Ryan and Louch. As I have indicated earlier, Mill also, however, employs the term "interests" in contexts where he links interests with rights. It is failure to take account of these contexts that consitutes the earlier-mentioned deficiency in the Ryan-Louch analysis. What I shall argue is that when Mill links interests with rights the interests he invokes are the "permanent" or "essential" interests of man. And this makes an important difference to the way his liberty-limiting principle is to be understood.

My examination of Mill's account of justice in *Utilitarianism* indicated he regards the rules of justice as a subclass of the rules of morality, but as "incomparably the most sacred and binding part, of all morality."[31] Since the rules of justice concern any and every man's well-being more closely than any other moral rules, everyone has the strongest interest in seeing

---
[29] "If any one does an act hurtful to others, there is a *prima facie* case for punishing him, by law, or, where legal penalties are not safely applicable by general disapprobation." OL, p.74. Cp. p.132.
[30] Ryan, *op.cit.*, p.620.
[31] U, p.55.

them maintained. Further, because the duties correlated with the fundamental rights of justice are of more absolute obligation than other moral rules, they may properly be upheld by "sterner" sanctions.[32] It is, I submit, Mill's stress on the overwhelming importance of rules of justice that leads him in *On Liberty* to emphasise the close link between interests and rights in certain of his formulations, explanations and applications of the principle of self-protection.

Mill's emphasis on rights and interests is, moreover, closely connected with his stress on the value of moral consensus (remarked on earlier[33]). Briefly put, his contention is that earlier Benthamite liberalism had been altogether one-sided in neglecting the need for a certain sort of moral consensus within a liberal society. Without such a consensus liberty and individuality cannot flourish and develop. What Mill wanted was unity in part of the moral sphere, namely in the sphere of just, other-regarding actions; but diversity of taste, conduct and belief in the spheres of the prudential and the aesthetic or noble - the areas, that is to say, of self-regarding actions. Given a firm framework of certain fundamental moral beliefs it would then be possible for men and women freely to pursue their own lines of conduct and to develop their personal ideals. "Personal interests and feelings, in the social state, can only obtain the maximum of satisfaction by means of co-operation, and the necessary condition of co-operation is a common belief. All human society, consequently is grounded on a system of fundamental opinions..."[34] The most essential part of the moral framework is made up of the rules of justice. These are the "moral rules which forbid mankind to hurt one another," among which we must always include "wrongful interference with each other's freedom". They are "the main element in determining the whole of the social feelings of mankind" and it is their observance above all which preserves social peace and allows everyone to obtain his fair share of happiness.[35] Or, as he states elsewhere, men attain most happiness "when each pursues his own, under the rules and conditions required by the good of the rest..."[36]

---

[32] *Ibid.*, p.60.
[33] See Chapter I.
[34] *Auguste Comte and Positivism, op.cit.*, p.101, cf. p.103; cf. "Coleridge", *op.cit.*, pp.136-37; *Logic, op.cit.*, p.601.
[35] U, p.55.
[36] *Auguste Comte and Positivism, op.cit.*, p.141. See also pp.142-44.

In *On Liberty* too, there are systematic manifestations of Mill's belief in the overwhelming importance of the rules of justice as prerequisites of freedom. Mill's liberty-limiting principle was designed to promote and protect man's interests in two distinct ways. First, there is the absolute prohibition of interference with self-regarding conduct. The purpose of this is to allow individuality to flourish by protecting men against any constraint whatever in the self-regarding area and especially against what Mill regarded as a salient contemporary menace, namely paternalistic constraints, interference with people 'for their own good'. Then, secondly, there is the prohibition of conduct which can only be engaged in at the expense of the interests of others. Among men's interests Mill was particularly concerned to protect their permanent interests, that is to say the rights dictated by justice. In Chapter III of his essay, Mill says that "As much compression as is necessary to prevent the stronger specimens of human nature from enroaching on the rights of others *cannot be dispensed with.*" [37] And he then goes on to describe freedom of action as being "held to rigid rules of justice for the sake of others."[38] A little earlier in the same chapter, he has been maintaining that individuality should be cultivated "within the limits imposed by the rights and interests of others."[39] Further, in Chapter II of his essay, in what is evidently a careful formulation of his principle, Mill once more explicitly refers to the rights dictated by justice. He contends that even though society was not founded on a contract,

> "every one who receives the protection of society owes a return for the benefit, and the fact of living in society renders it *indispensable* that each should be bound to observe a certain line of conduct towards the rest. This conduct consists, first, in not injuring the interests of one another; or rather certain interests, which, either by express legal provision or by tacit understanding, ought to be considered as rights; and secondly, in each person's bearing his share. . . of the labours and sacrifices incurred for defending the society and its members from injury and molestation. These conditions society is *justified in enforcing, at all costs* to those who endeavour to withhold fulfilment."[40]

---

[37] OL, p.121. My emphasis.
[38] *Ibid.*, p.121.
[39] *Ibid.*, p.120.
[40] *Ibid.*, p.132. My italics.

Mill is arguing that every man by virtue of living in society incurs certain "paramount" obligations.[41] These are, first, a duty not to damage the permanent interests or violate the fundamental rights of others (ie. the rights of justice). Thus if we cause a man bodily harm, rob him of his property, interfere with his freedom, break a contract or an engagement we have made with him or infringe any of his legal rights we may be said to have treated him *unjustly*. Secondly, any person may rightfully be compelled to carry out certain *positive* actions "necessary to the interest of the society of which he enjoys the protection."[42] He may, for instance, legitimately be obliged to defend his country against an external aggressor or to give evidence in a court of law. Society is justified in enforcing these obligations "at all costs". If we fail to fulfil them we may properly incur severe punishment, by law where appropriate or by social opinion where legal penalties would be inexpedient. Where unjust conduct consists in the violation of a person's legal, or "constituted rights", he may obviously be punished by the sanctions of the law. Mill also evidently commits himself to the use of legal sanctions against those who fail to fulfil their positive obligations towards society.[43]

What I have shown here is that Mill takes unjust conduct, i.e. interference with the rights or permanent interests of others, to be less than the whole of other-regarding conduct, albeit the part he is most concerned with. When other-regarding conduct prejudices the "immediate" interests of others - injures or harms them in some way - there is a *prima facie* case for legal or social restraint. Unjust other-regarding conduct on the other hand, since it damages men's permanent interests, absolutely requires to be controlled and hence is subject to appropriately severe sanctions.[44]

To show that conduct affects prejudicially the interests of others, that it harms or injures them in some way, is only to have made out a *prima facie* case for either legal or social control. To show that conduct harms others is necessary but not sufficient to demonstrate that it should be subject to legal or social sanctions; "it must by no means be supposed, because damage, or probability of damage, to the interests of others, can alone justify the

---

[41] Cf. U, p.59.
[42] OL, p.74.
[43] *Ibid.*, p.74.
[44] *Ibid.*, pp.114,121,132; U, p.60.

interference of society, that therefore it always does justify such interference."[45]   In competitive situations, for instance, we may cause others to suffer acute disappointment by preventing them from securing some good they had a reasonable chance of obtaining. But it is better for the "general interest" that neither state nor society should intervene in order to relieve unsuccessful competitors from this sort of suffering. Even when, in principle, conduct is seen to be other-regarding we have still to consider whether or not it is for the greatest happiness of mankind that we should interfere. As Mill explains it earlier in his essay, ". . . the question whether the general welfare will or will not be promoted by interfering with it (other-regarding conduct), becomes open to discussion."[46]

In short, there may well be utilitarian arguments against interference with other-regarding conduct and these have to be met and overcome by those who would argue for social or legal prohibition. Now, my contention is that where *unjust* other-regarding conduct is concerned such arguments against interference cannot in Mill's view be invoked. To show that other-regarding conduct violates the fundamental rights of others is sufficient to justify prohibiting it. Consider again Mill's discussion of competitive situations. He urges that there should be no intervention in such cases. Why? Because "society admits no right, either legal or moral, in the disappointed competitors to immunity from this kind of suffereng; and feels called upon to interfere, only when means of success have been employed which it is contrary to the general interest to permit - namely, fraud, or treachery, and force."[47] The general welfare would thus be promoted by intervention in such a case only when the competitors had breached one or more of the principles of justice - the moral rules against such things as force, fraud, treachery, which concern "the essentials of human well-being" much more than any others and which mankind has the strongest interest in enforcing.

---

[45] OL, p.150. As he puts it elsewhere: "Even in those portions of conduct which do affect the interest of others, the onus of making out a case always lies on the defenders of legal prohibition. It is not a merely constructive or presumptive injury to others, which will justify the interference of law with individual freedom." PPE, p.569.
[46] OL, p.132.
[47] *Ibid.,* p.150.

Again, trade is a "social act" and so, in principle, may endanger or damage the interests of others. In discussing whether trading should indeed be controlled Mill claims that there is a clear case for regulation in the general interest where combination among manufacturers or retailers restricts "the equal freedom" of buyers for supplying themselves from other sources or where it is necessary to protect the public against fraud by adulteration or to protect workers in dangerous occupations.[48]

These particular arguments of Mill's show him applying the following principles of argument: where interests are prejudicially affected, the agent is liable to punishment and it is a matter of utilitarian expediency whether some (legal or social) sanction is best invoked or not. But in the case of a specifically *unjust* action, invoking of some sanction is always appropriate.

The permanent interests protected by rules of justice may be, indeed normally are, *socially recognised* or *established* interests. Thus it is generally reckoned unjust to break faith with anyone, to treat him unfairly, or to deprive him of his personal liberty or property. More positively, it is customarily assumed that a person ought not to receive the protection afforded by society without bearing his "fair share" in the defence of his country and so forth. But it should be emphasised that there is a misleading element in those occasional passages where Mill writes as if his principle refers only to socially established permanent interests (e.g. where he speaks of the infringement of "constituted rights"). There is no conflict between this way of talking and his basic position in those standard cases where permanent interests and socially recognised interests coincide. But in examining the fundamentals of his position it should be borne in mind that his basic appeal is to permanent interests which "ought to be considered as rights" - i.e. so considered not because they have received social recognition but because they are in accordance with the dictates of justice.

Just as Mill is concerned to demand absolute immunity from interference for self-regarding actions, so, it can now be seen, he is prepared to argue conversely that an important part of other-regarding conduct requires absolutely to be controlled. A man's conduct may, indeed,

---
[48] *Ibid.*, pp.150-151.

be seen as susceptible of being brought under a hierarchy of considerations relating him to liability to coercion or punishment. The self-regarding aspects of his conduct are immune from considerations of punishment. But should his conduct also have other-regarding aspects, he brings himself into the area of operation of morality, perhaps of law, and loses his immunity to coercion and punishment. Society may then control him. Should the other-regarding aspects of his conduct be such as to breach the permanent interests of others, he then makes himself subject to considerations of justice and thus brings himself into the area where it is absolutely necessary for society to exercise stringent control.

If each man is to exercise his individuality and so develop his higher capacities, he must, as a general rule, be free of interference - including interference designed 'for his own good'. He must be allowed a self-regarding realm in which to achieve his ideals of personal excellence. Equally, if others are to be self-determining and to develop their potentialities, each man must be induced to respect the interests of others. Most vital of all, each man must be restrained from violating the fundamental rights of any other, (especially his right to equal freedom). There must be stringent control of those of his other-regarding actions which are not only immoral but also unjust. Only under such limitations can each man have secured to him his liberty.

BIBLIOGRAPHY

I. WORKS OF JOHN STUART MILL

A System of Logic: London: Longmans, 1949.

Principles of Political Economy: London: Longmans, Green, Reader and Dyer, 1866.

Utilitarianism, Liberty, Representative Government: London: J.M. Dent & Sons, Everyman edition, 1910.

Dissertations and Discussions (4 Vols.): London: Longmans, Green, Reader and Dyer, 1875.

On the Subjection of Women: London: Dent, Everyman edition, 1929.

Collected Works of John Stuart Mill: General Editor, P.E.L. Priestley: Canada: University of Toronto Press:

> Vols. II and III, *Principles of Political Economy* (ed. J.M. Robson), 1965.

> Vols. IV and V, *Essays on Economics and Society* (ed. J.M. Robson), 1967.

> Vols. XII and XIII, *The Earlier Letters of John Stuart Mill* (ed. F. Mineka), 1963.

Auguste Comte and Positivism: Michigan: University of Michigan Press, 1961.

Chapters onSocialism (ed. W.D.P. Bliss): New York: 1891.

Autobiography of John Stuart Mill: New York: Columbia University Press, 1924.

The Early Draft of J.S. Mill's Autobiography (ed. Jack Stillinger): Urbana: University of Illinois Press, 1961.

An Examination of Sir William Hamilton's Philosophy: London: Longmans, Green, Reader and Dyer, 1872.

Nature and Utility of Religion (ed. G. Nakhnikian): New York: The Bobbs-Merrill Co., 1958.

Letters of John Stuart Mill (ed. H.S.R. Elliot), (2 Vols): London: Longmans, Green, 1910.

The Spirit of the Age (ed. F.A. Hayek): Chicago: University of Chicago Press, 1942.

Essays on Politics and Culture (ed. G. Himmelfarb): New York: Anchor Books, 1963.

Six Great Humanistic Essays of John Stuart Mill (ed. A.W. Levi): New York: Washington Square Press, 1963.

Mill's Ethical Writings (ed. J.B. Schneewind): New York: Collier Books, 1965.

Mill's Essays on Literature and Society (ed. J.B. Schneewind): New York: Collier Books, 1965.

John Stuart Mill: Literary Essays (ed. E. Alexander): New York: The Bobbs-Merrill Co., 1967.

II. OTHER WORKS:

Adler, Mortimer: *The Idea of Freedom:* New York: Doubleday, Vol.I, 1958; Vol.II, 1961.

Alexander, Edward: *Matthew Arnold and John Stuart Mill:* London: Routledge and Kegan Paul, 1965.

Anschutz, R.F: *The Philosophy of J.S. Mill:* Oxford: Oxford University Press, 1953.

Austin, Jean: "Pleasure and Happiness", *Philosophy,* Vol.XLIII, No.163 (January, 1968).

Bain, A: *John Stuart Mill:* London: Longmans, Green, 1882.

Bay, Christian: *The Structure of Freedom:* Stanford: Stanford University Press, 1958.

Barry, Brian: *Political Argument:* London: Routledge and Keegan Paul, 1965.

Benn, S.I. and Peters, R.S: *Social Principles and the Democratic State:* London: George Allen and Unwin, 1959.

Benn, S.I: " 'Interests' in Politics", *Proceedings of the Aristotelian Society* (1959-60).

------------ : "Rights", *The Encyclopedia of Philosophy* (ed. Paul Edwards): New York: Collier Macmillan, 1967.

------------ : "Nature of Political Philosophy", under *Political Philosophy* in *The Encyclopedia of Philosophy* (ed. Paul Edwards): New York: Collier Macmillan, 1967.

------------ : "Freedom and Persuasion", *Australasian Journal of Philosophy,* Vol.45, No.3 (December, 1967).

Bentham, Jeremy: *A Fragment on Government* (ed. W. Harrison): Oxford: Basil Blackwell, 1960.

------------ : *The Principles of Morals and Legislation* (ed. Wilfred Harrison): Oxford: Basil Blackwell, 1960.

Berlin, I: *J.S. Mill and the Ends of Life:* London: The Council of Christians and Jews, 1959.

---------- : *Two Concepts of Liberty:* Oxford: Oxford University Press, 1958.

Bosanquet, Bernard: *The Philosophical Theory of the State:* London: Macmillan, 1923.

Bradley, F.H: *Ethical Studies:* Oxford: Oxford University Press, 1876.

Brandt, Richard B. (ed.): *Social Justice:* Englewood Cliffs, N.J: Prentice Halll, 1962.

Britton, Karl: *John Stuart Mill:* London: Penguin Books, 1953.

-------------- : "Utilitarianism: The Appeal to a First Principle", *Proceedings of the Aristotelian Society* (1959-60).

Burns, J.H: "J.S. Mill and Democracy, 1829-61", *Political Studies,* Vol.V, Part I in No.2; Part II in No.3 (1957).

------------- : "Utilitarianism and Democracy", *Philosophical Quarterly,* Vol.9, 1959.

Cranston, Maurice: *Freedom: A New Analysis:* London: Longmans, Green, 1953.

------------- : " 'Mill on Liberty': A Revaluation", *The Listener* (January 10, 1957).

------------- : *John Stuart Mill:* London: Longmans, Green for the British Council, 1958.

------------- : *Human Rights To-day:* London: Ampersand Books, 1962.

------------- (ed.): *Western Political Philosophers:* London: The Bodley Head, 1966.

------------ : "Toleration", *The Encyclopedia of Philosophy* (ed. Paul Edwards): New York: Collier Macmillan, 1967.

------------ : *Political Dialogues:* London: British Broadcasting Corporation, 1968.

Cowling, M: *Mill and Liberalism:* Cambridge: Cambridge University Press, 1963.

Day, J.P; "John Stuart Mill", *A Critical History of Western Philosophy* (ed. D.J. O'Connor): London: The Free Press of Glencoe, Collier-Macmillan, 1964.

Devlin, The Hon. Sir Patrick: *The Enforcement of Morals* (Maccabaean Lecture in Jurisprudence of the British Academy): London: Oxford University Press for the British Academy, 1959.

Downie, R.S: "Mill on Pleasure and Self-Development", *Philosophical Quarterly,* Vol.16, No.62 (1966).

---------------- : *Government Action and Morality:* London: Macmillan, 1964.

Eisenberg, Paul. D: "Duties to Oneself and the Concept of Morality:, *Inquiry,* 11 (1968).

Frankel, Charles: *The Case for Modern Man:* New York: Harper and Brothers, 1955.

---------------- : *The Love of Anxiety:* New York: Harper and Brothers, 1965.

---------------- : "The Idea of Progress", under *Progress* in *The Encyclopedia of Philosophy* (ed. Paul Edwards): New York: Collier Macmillan, 1967.

Friedman, Richard B: "A New Exploration of Mill's Essay *On Liberty*", *Political Studies,* Vol.14, No.3 (1966).

Friedrich, Carl J. (ed.): *Liberty* (*Nomos IV*): New York: Atherton Press, 1962.

Fromm, E: *Fear of Freedom:* London: Routledge and Kegan Paul, 1960.

Gellner, E: *Thought and Change:* London: Weidenfeld and Nicolson, 1964.

Ginsberg, M: *On the Diversity of Morals:* London: Heinemann, 1956.

Greaves, H.G.R: *The Foundations of Political Theory:* London: George Allen and Unwin, 1958.

Halevy, Elie: *The Growth of Philosophic Radicalism:* London: Faber & Faber, 1949.

Halliday, R.J: "Some Recent Interpretations of John Stuart Mill", *Philosophy,* Vol.XLIII, no.163 (January, 1968).

Hamburger, Joseph: *Intellectuals in Politics:* New Haven: Yale University Press, 1966.

Hampshire, Stuart: "Human Nature in Politics:, *The Listener* (December 3, 1953).

--------------- : "Uncertainty in Politics", *Encounter,* Vol.VIII, No.1 (January, 1957).

--------------- : *Spinoza and the Idea of Freedom,* Dawes Hicks Lecture on Philosophy, British Academy, 1960 (Monograph version reprinted from the Proceedings of the British Academy, Vol.XLVI): London: Oxford University Press.

--------------- : *Thought and Action:* London: Chatto and Windus, 1960.

Hare, R.M: *Freedom and Reason:* Oxford at the Clarendon Press, 1965.

Harris, Abram L: "John Stuart Mill's Theory of Progress", *Ethics*, Vol.LXVI, No.3 (April,1956).

Hart, H.L.A: *Bentham:* (from the Proceedings of the British Academy, Vol.XLVIII): London: Oxford University Press, 1962

--------------- : *The Concept of Law:* Oxford at the Clarendon Press, 1963.

--------------- : *Law, Liberty and Morality:* Stanford University Press, 1963.

Hayek, F.A: *John Stuart Mill and Harriet Taylor:* London: Routledge and Kegan Paul, 1951.

--------------- : *The Constitution of Liberty:* London: Routledge and Kegan Paul, 1960.

Hobhouse, L.T: *Liberalism:* London: Williams and Norgate, 1910.

Honderich, Ted: "Mill on Liberty", *Inquiry,* 10 (1967).

von Humboldt, Wilhelm: *The Sphere and Duties of Government,* trans. Coulthard: 1854.

Mill, James: *An Essay on Government* in *Essays:* London: n.p.n.d.

Laslett, Peter (ed.): *Philosophy, Politics and Society:* Oxford: Basil Blackwell, 1956.

------------------ and Runciman, W.G. (eds.): *Philosophy, Politics and Society: Second Series:* Oxford: Basil Blackwell, 1962.

------------------ and --------------------- (eds.): *Philosophy, Politics and Society: Third Series:* Oxford: Basil Blackwell, 1967.

Levi, Albert William: "The Value of Freedom: Mill's Liberty (1859-1959)", *Ethics* (October, 1959).

Letwin, Shirley Robin: *The Pursuit of Certainty:* Cambridge: Cambridge University Press, 1965.

Louch, A.R.: "Sins and Crimes", *Philosophy,* Vol.XLIII, No.163 (January, 1968).

Lucas, J.R: *The Principles of Politics:* Oxford: Clarendon Press, 1966.

Lichtman, Richard: "The Surface and Substance of Mill's Defence of Freedom", *Social Research,* Vol.30 (Winter, 1963).

McCloskey, H.J: "The State and Evil", *Ethics,* LXIX, 3 (April, 1959).

-------------------- : "Practical Implications of the State's Right to Promote the Good", *Ethics,* LXXI, 2 (1961).

-------------------- : "Mill's Liberalism", *Philosophical Quarterly,* Vol.13 (April, 1963).

-------------------- : "A Critique of the Ideals of Liberty", *Mind,* Vol.LXXIV, No.296 (October, 1965).

-------------------- : "Immorality, Indecency and the Law", *Political Studies,* Vol.XIII, No.3 (October, 1965).

-------------------- : "The Problem of Liberalism", *Review of Metaphysics,* Vol.19 (1965-66).

-------------------- : "Mill's Liberalism - A Rejoinder to Mr. Ryan", *Philosophical Quarterly,* Vol.16, No.62, (1966).

-------------------- : "Some Arguments for a Liberal Society", *Philosophy,* Vol.XLIII, no.166 (October, 1968).

MacIntyre, A.C: *A Short History of Ethics:* New York: Macmillan, 1966.

Mandelbaum, Maurice: "On Interpreting Mill's *Utilitarianism*", *Journal of the History of Philosophy,* Vol.VI, No.1 (January, 1968).

Monro, D.H: Reviews of *The Nature and Limits of Political Science* and *Mill and Liberalism,* both by Maurice Cowling; *Australasian Journal of Philosophy,* Vol.42 (1964).

--------------- : "Jeremy Bentham", *The Encyclopedia of Philosophy* (ed. Paul Edwards): New York: Collier Macmillan, 1967.

Mueller, Iris W: *John Stuart Mill and French Thought:* Urbana: University of Illinois Press, 1956.

Oakeshott, Michael: "The Masses in Representative Democracy", *Freedom and Serfdom* (ed. Albert Hunold): Dordrecht, Holland: D. Reidel Publishing Co. (1961).

------------------ : *Rationalism in Politics and Other Essays:* London: Menthuen, 1967.

Oppenheim, Felix E: *Dimensions of Freedom:* New York: St. Martin's Press, 1961.

Packe, M.St.J: *The Life of John Stuart Mill:* London: Secker and Warburg, 1954.

Pappe, H.O: *J.S. Mill and the Harriet Taylor Myth:* Melbourne: Melbourne University Press, 1960.

Partridge, P.H: *Thinking About Politics:* Canberra: The Australian National University, 1956.

------------------ : *On Liberty - a J.S. Mill Centenary:* Sydney: Department of Tutorial Classes, University of Sydney, 1958.

------------------ : "Politics, Philosophy, Ideology", *Political Studies,* Vol.9 (1961).

------------------ : "Hayek on Law and Liberty", *The Indian Journal of Philosophy,* Vol.IV, No.11 (January, 1964).

------------------ : "Political Philosophy and Political Sociology", *Australian and New Zealand Journal of Sociology,* Vol.I, (April, 1965).

------------------ : "Freedom", *The Encyclopedia of Philosophy* (ed. Paul Edwards): New York: Collier Macmillan, 1967.

Passmore, J.A: *A Hundred Years of Philosophy:* London: Duckworth, 1957.

Plamenatz, John: "Interests", *Political Studies,* Vol.II (1954).

------------------ : *The English Utilitarians:* Oxford: Basil Blackwell, 1958.

------------------ : "The Legacy of Philosophical Radicalism", in *Law and Opinion in England in the 20th Century* (ed. M. Ginsberg): London: Stevens & Sons, 1959.

------------------ : "The Use of Political Theory", *Political Studies,* Vol.VIII (1960).

------------------ : *Man and Society* (Volume Two): London: Longmans, 1963.

------------------ : *Readings from Liberal Writers:* London: George Allen and Unwin, 1965.

Peters, R.S: *Ethics and Education:* London: George Allen and Unwin, 1966.

Quinton, Anthony (ed.): *Political Philosophy:* Oxford: Oxford University Press, 1967.

Radcliff, Peter (ed.): *Limits of Liberty: Studies of Mill's* On Liberty: Belmont, California: Wadsworth, 1966.

Raphael, D. Daiches: "Fallacies In and About Mill's *Utilitarianism*", *Philosophy,* Vol.XXX (1955).

------------------ (ed.): *Political Theory and the Rights of Man:* London: Macmillan, 1967.

Rees, J.C: "The Limitations of Political Theory", *Political Studies,* Vol.II (1954).

------------ : *Mill and His Early Critics:* Leicester: Leicester University Press, 1956.

------------ : "A Phase in the Development of Mill's Ideas on Liberty", *Political Studies,* Vol.VI, No.1 (1958).

------------ : "A Re-Reading of Mill on Liberty", *Political Studies,* Vol.VIII, No.2 (1960).

------------ : "Individualism and Individual Liberty", *Il Politico,* Vol.26 (1961).

------------ : "Hayek on Liberty", *Philosophy,* Vol.XXXVIII, No.146 (October, 1963).

------------ : "Was Mill for Liberty?", *Political Studies,* Vol.XIV (1966).

------------ : "John Stuart Mill: I. Political Contributions", *International Encyclopedia of the Social Sciences* (ed. David I. Sills): New York: Collier Macmillan, 1968.

Ritchie, D.G: *The Principles of State Interference:* London: Swan Sonneneschein & Co., 1891.

de Ruggiero, Guido: *The History of European Liberalism* (trans. by R.G. Collingwood): Boston: Beacon Press, 1964.

Ryan, Alan: "Mr. McCloskey on Mill's Liberalism", *Philosophical Quarterly,* Vol.14, No.56 (July, 1964).

-------------- : "John Stuart Mill", *New Society* (22nd October, 1964).

---------- : "John Stuart Mill's Art of Living", *The Listener* (October, 1965).

Sabine, George H: *A History of Political Theory* (Third Edition): London: George G. Harrap, 1963.

Schneewind, J.B: "John Stuart Mill", *The Encyclopedia of Philosophy* (ed. Paul Edwards): New York: Collier Macmillan, 1967.

Scott, K.J: "Conditioning and Freedom", *Australasian Journal of Philosophy,* Vol.37 (1959).

Shils, Edward: "The Theory of Mass Society", *Diogenes,* No.39, (Fall, 1962).

Spence, G.W: "The Psychology Behind J.S. Mill's 'Proof' ", *Philosophy,* Vol.XLIII, No.163 (January, 1968).

Strawson, P.F: "Social Morality and Individual Ideal", *Philosophy,* Vol.XXXVI, No.136 (January, 1961).

Stephen, Sir James Fitz-James: *Liberty, Equality, Fraternity:* London: Smith, Elder & Co., 1873.

Stephen, Sir Leslie: *The English Utilitarians: Vol.3: John Stuart Mill:* London: Duckworth & Co., 1900.

Street, C.L: *Individualism and Individuality in the Philsophy of John Stuart Mill:* Milwaukee: Morehouse Publishing Co., 1926.

Taylor, Gabriele and Wolfram, Sybil: "Mill, Punishment and the Self-Regarding Failings", *Analysis,* Vol.28, No.5 (n.s. No.125) (April, 1968).

------------------- and ------------------ : "The Self-Regarding and Other-Regarding Virtues", *The Philosophical Quarterly,* Vol.18, No.72 (July, 1968).

Ten, C.L: "Mill on Self-Regarding Actions", *Philosophy,* Vol.XLIII, No.163 (January, 1968).

de Tocqueville, Alexis: *Democracy in America:* London: Oxford University Press, 1953.

Thompson, E.P. (ed.): *Out of Apathy:* London: Stevens and Sons, 1960.

Thomson, David (ed.): *Political Ideas:* London: C.A. Watts, 1966.

Weinstein, W.L: "The Concept of Liberty in Nineteenth Century English Political Thought", *Political Studies,* Vol.XIII (1965).

Weldon, T.D: *The Vocabulary of Politics:* London: Penguin Books, 1953.

West, E.G: "Liberty and Education; John Stuart Mill's Dilemma", *Philosophy,* Vol.XL, No.152 (April, 1965).

Willey, Basil: *Nineteenth-Century Studies:* London: Penguin Books in Association with Chatto and Windus, 1964.

Williams, Bernard: "Democracy and Ideology", *The Political Quarterly,* Vol.32 (1961).

--------------------- and Montefiore, A. (eds.): *British Analytical Philosophy:* London: Routledge and Kegan Paul, 1966.

Wilson, John: *Equality:* London: Hutchinson, 1966.

Wolin, Sheldon S: *Politics and Vision:* London: George Allen & Unwin, 1961.